Bilingual
Guide
to Japan

WASHOKU SEASONING

MATSUDA Michiko

Photography by NABESHIMA Naruyasu

SHOGAKUKAN

Bilingual Guide to Japan
WASHOKU SEASONING

MATSUDA Michiko
Photography by NABESHIMA Naruyasu

Book and Cover design ©Kindaichi Design
English Translation ©Active Gaming Madia,
Jeannine Law-Smith

Published by
SHOGAKUKAN
2-3-1 Hitotsubashi Chiyoda-Ku,
Tokyo 101-8001 JAPAN
tel : +81-3-3230-5119
fax : +81-3-5226-7847
http://www.shogakukan.co.jp

WASHOKU CHOMIRYO BILINGUAL GUIDE by
MATSUDA Michiko, NABESHIMA Naruyasu
©2016 MATSUDA Michiko, NABESHIMA Naruyasu,
KOMATSU Hiroko ╱ SHOGAKUKAN
Printed in Japan
ISBN 978-4-09-388531-7

和食調味料バイリンガルガイド

松田美智子 監修

鍋島徳恭 写真

小学館

English Renderings of Cooking Terms

This English and Japanese bilingual book introduces the basic knowledge and representative recipes of *Washoku* (Japanese food) seasonings.

All Japanese terms are rendered in Italicized Roman characters. The only diacritical marks used are the macron (ˉ), to indicate long vowel sounds, and the hyphen (-), to separate two adjacent vowel sounds.

Since the conventions for rendering these terms into English differ depending on the region, terms used elsewhere may not be consistent with those used in this book. Given that even Japanese names and pronunciations may differ depending on the region, they cannot be generalized. Standard names are used in this book and are rendered so that they can be easily read by individuals who are not native speakers of Japanese.

Many ingredients are not available outside of Japan. In order to allow as many people as possible to experience these flavors overseas, the most commonly-available ingredients and cooking tools are listed in sections of this book that contain recipes. For example, in fluid measures, 1 cup = 240ml (U.S. standard).

本書の英文表記について

この本は、代表的な和食調味料について紹介しています。日本語が母語ではない人のために、英語で訳してあります。日本語はすべてローマ字読みにし、斜体のアルファベットで表記しています。発音は長音記号マクロン (ˉ) のみ表記し、母音が続いてしまう場合のみハイフン (ー) を使用しています。

※これら外国語表記は、地方により異なるルールで表記されているため、本書と一致しない場合があります。特に固有名称とその発音については、地方によって日本語でも呼び方が異なることがあり、一般化はできません。本書では標準的な呼称を掲載し、外国語を母語とする読者ができるだけ平易に発音できる表記としました。

※海外で入手できない和食材料や調理器具は多々あります。より多くの外国居住者の方が実践できるよう、レシピの章ではできるだけ一般的なものをあえて使用しています。なお、1カップ＝200ml（和文）、1cup＝240ml（英文）で表記しています。

Table of Contents 目次

Introduction

Seasonings are the foundations of *washoku*

For the Japanese, the term "*washoku*" refers to everyday homemade Japanese cooking. However, for the rest of the world it is evolving into a much greater concept. It is appreciated as a "food culture" more than ever since it was registered on the list of UNESCO Intangible Cultural World Heritages in 2013. Because of this and its health benefits, an increasing number of foreigners want to make simple *washoku* in their own homes.

As part of my work as a food researcher, I have an ever-increasing number of chances to teach Japanese home cooking to people overseas. In facing the difficulties of explaining food from a foreign culture, I noted the importance of understanding seasoning intently. This understanding is vital when explaining "uniquely Japanese flavor," because Japanese flavors can only be created with traditional Japanese seasonings - such as soy sauce, *miso*, and *mirin*.

These traditional Japanese seasonings were all born among Japan's four distinct seasons and natural landscape. Even the soy sauce and *miso* sold at global supermarkets these days are fermented seasonings made from *koji*, a chance byproduct of *sake* brewing. As such, they were born against the backdrop of a rich food culture. Furthermore, their uses in the culinary arts have

はじめに

● 調味料こそ和食の基本

「和食」というと、日本人の我々にとっては家庭で日常食べる日本料理ですが、2014年ユネスコ世界無形文化遺産に登録され、「食文化」としての価値が一層見直されています。健康的であるという観点からも、料理研究家として海外の方へ日本の家庭料理を教える機会は増える一方です。異文化である料理を理解してもらう難しさに向き合うなかで、"日本ならではの味わい"を伝えるためには、調味料を理解することが重要であることに改めて気づかされました。なぜなら、醤油、味噌、みりんといった日本固有の調味料があって、初めて日本の味を組み立てることができるからです。それら日本固有の調味料は、いずれも「日本の四季」「風土」の中で生まれたものです。

also developed. For example, into the basic method of adding soy sauce to *sashimi*, as well as into intricate combinations with other seasonings and *dashi* to make *tare* and *tsuyu*. And above all else, they developed into the means of seasoning world-famous representatives of *washoku* like *teriyaki* and *tempura*.

The importance of "sa-shi-su-se-so"

When teaching about food, I always do my best to pass on traditional home cooking through my own filter, in a way that suits the times. I think the use of seasoning is a good example of that method.

The sounds "sa-shi-su-se-so" are characters taken one each from *satō* (sugar), *shio* (salt), *su* (vinegar), *seuyu* (soy sauce or *shoyu* in an archaic pronunciation), and *miso*. This is a saying I learned from my mother and grandmother about the order to add seasonings. I am sure that many people follow this practice without really thinking about the reasons for it, but sugar is added before salt because its particles are larger. The salt will fill up the gaps in the fibers of the ingredients if it is added first, and the sugar will not be able to fit in. Soy sauce and *miso* are added last to keep their aromas from being lost. That old oral tradition of "sa-shi-su-se-so" actually contains a scientific element that

いまや世界中のスーパーで売られている醤油や味噌も、酒造りの偶然の産物である「麹」を用いた発酵調味であり、豊かな食文化が背景にあってこそ誕生したものです。さらに、その使い方においても、たとえば刺身に醤油をつけるといった基本の使い方はもちろん、他の調味料やだしと複合的に組み合わせることで「たれ」や「つゆ」になり、それらを利用した調理法で、世界中で愛される「照り焼き」「天ぷら」といった代表的な和食へと発展してきたのです。

●「さ・し・す・せ・そ」の大切さ

料理を教えるときにいつも心がけていることの一つが、伝承された家庭料理を、私なりのフィルターを通して、「今の時代にあった形で伝える」ということです。調味料の使い方はその良い例だといえます。砂糖、塩、酢、醤油（せうゆ）、味噌のから一文字

carries on in Japanese cooking even in modern times.

If you learn the origins of these traditional Japanese seasonings and grasp their virtues and uses, you can follow the framework of Japanese cooking. Whether you're bringing foreign guests to a high-class restaurant or making a simple dish for the dinner table at home, this book contains the foundations for properly enjoying *washoku*.

Michiko Matsuda
Culinary Researcher

ずっとった「さ・し・す・せ・そ」。これは、母や祖母に教わった、調味料を加える順番を指し示した諺です。特に理由を考えずに実践している方も多くいらっしゃるかと思いますが、砂糖を先に加えるのは塩より粒子が大きいためで、先に塩を入れると素材の繊維の隙間が塩で埋まり、砂糖が入らなくなってしまうからなのです。醤油や味噌を最後に加えるのは、香りが飛ばないようにするため。昔ながらの言い伝えである「さ・し・す・せ・そ」には、実は現代にも通じる日本料理の科学的な側面が込められていたのです。これら日本固有の調味料の成り立ちを学び、効能や使い方を知れば、日本の料理の骨格をたどることができます。外国人の方を連れて高級店に食べに行くにも、あるいは日々の家庭の食卓にのぼるちょっとした一品を作るのにも、和食を正しく楽しむための調味料の基礎を、この一冊にまとめました。

（料理研究家　松田美智子）

Chapter 1

Basic
Seasonings

第一章

基本調味料

Satō

There are six types of *satō* (sugar in Japanese) commonly used in Japan: *granyu-tō* (granulated sugar), *johakutō*, *zarame*, *san'on-tō*, *koku-tō*, and *wasanbon-tō*. *Satō* is made by boiling down juice squeezed from plants like the sugar beet and can be divided into a number of different types based on whether it was created directly from the juice and contains molasses (a non-centrifugal sugar, or *ganmitsu-tō*) or treated with a centrifuge to remove the molasses (a centrifugal sugar, or *bunmitsu-tō*). Increasing purity allows for the further creation of a wide variety of sugars. The first crystallization creates *granyu-tō*, which is the purest of the sugars and suitable for confectionary applications. Created from the remaining solution, *johakutō* is moist, soft, and works well in the simmered dishes of Japanese cuisine. *San'on-tō* is made with the liquid left over from *johakutō* and has a somewhat higher mineral content as well as a sweet flavor with *ki-re* (p. 106) and *koku* (p. 106). The sugar liquid is separated even further and heated over and over again to create distinctly colored *zarame*, which is notable for its aroma and *koku*. This sugar's granules are quite large and melt slowly, making it suitable for applications where one adds sugar content gradually, such as stewing large roasts. If there is one truly and uniquely Japanese sugar, it would be the *wasanbon-to* that is indispensable as an ingredient for Japanese sweets. Soaked and kneaded time and time again, *wasanbon-to* is composed of fine crystals that give this sugar its characteristic gentle, melt-in-your-mouth sweetness.

日本で一般的に使われている砂糖はグラニュー糖、上白糖、三温糖、ざらめ、和三盆糖、黒糖の6種。砂糖は、さとうきびなどの搾り汁を煮詰めてつくるが、煮詰めただけの「含蜜糖」（黒糖）と、搾り汁から遠心分離機などで糖蜜を分離させた「分蜜糖」に分かれ、さらにその純度を高めていくことでさまざまな砂糖となる。最初に結晶化した一番糖、グラニュー糖は、最も精製度が高く、結晶が細かく製菓向き。残った糖液からできる上白糖はしっとりソフトで日本料理の煮物に向く。三温糖は上白糖の残液を煮詰めたもので、ややミネラル分が多く、甘みにキレ (p.106) とコク (p.106) がある。さらに分離した蜜を何度も加熱することで色づいたのがざらめ。香りと独特のコクが特徴。粒子が大きいので溶けるのが遅く、ゆっくり糖分を含ませたい塊肉の煮物などに向く。日本ならではの砂糖といえば、和菓子の原料に欠かせない和三盆糖である。何度もさらしては練ることで、結晶が細かく、口どけのよさと淡い甘みが特徴。

Satō Uses

When making a simmered dish, sugar is usually added before salt because sugar grains are larger than salt grains. If salt is added first, the spaces between the fiber structures of the ingredients will become blocked with salt, making it difficult for sugar to penetrate. Also, sugar dehydrates through osmotic pressure just like salt does. For example, if you dust squash with sugar before simmering it, the sugar will remove some of the water content, opening up the plant fibers and allowing the broth to seep throughout the squash easily for a soft, gentle sweetness that only needs a little sugar.

Additionally, sugar is characterized by a steady sequence of temperature-dependent changes. Sugar mixed with water will steadily become stickier once heated over 100 °C (212 °F) until it becomes a toffee-like paste when heated to over 130 °C (266 °F). Once heated to over 160 °C (320 °F), the sugar will then begin to caramelize (p. 106). These changes in sugar are often used for confectionary purposes. Also, adding sugar to a beaten egg will allow the sugar to hold the air pockets created by the egg protein in place, making for thick and fluffy egg dishes.

　一般に煮物では、砂糖、塩の順に加えるが、これは、砂糖の粒子のほうが塩の粒子より大きいため、先に塩が入ると素材の繊維のすきまが塩で埋まってしまい、砂糖が中へ入りにくくなるのが理由。また、砂糖にも塩同様に浸透圧による脱水作用がある。例えばかぼちゃにまぶすと、水分が抜けて野菜の繊維が広がり、煮汁がすっと中に入り、少ない砂糖の量でほっくりと優しい甘さに煮上がる。

　温度によってどんどん状態が変化していくのも砂糖の特徴だ。水を加えた砂糖を加熱すると、100℃を超えると次第に粘りが強くなり、130℃を超えると飴状になる。さらに160℃を超えると、カラメル化 (p.106) する。製菓においては、こうした砂糖の変化を利用することも多い。また、溶いた卵液に砂糖を加えると、砂糖がたんぱく質の気泡をしっかり抱き込むので、空気を含んでふっくらとした焼き上がりになる。

Shio

Careful addition of *shio* (salt in Japanese) to enhance the flavor of food is a fundamental rule of cooking common to cuisines all across the globe. Though there are many different salts in the world, they can all be roughly broken into one of two categories: sea salt or *kai-en*, which is produced from the waters of the ocean, and rock salt or *gan-en*, which is mined from accumulations where sea water was sealed in the earth by crust movements and other geological phenomena.

Japan is surrounded by the ocean, and most of its salt is *kai-en*. Even among sea salts, *tenjitsu-en* (solar salt) is rich in minerals and other oceanic nutrients and is created simply through evaporation, for example in an *enden* (p. 107) or by boiling in a pot. *Tenjitsu-en* has a delicate saltiness with hints of sweet and savory flavors, making it our recommendation for seasoning food. There is also a kind of *tenjitsu-en* called *moshio* (seaweed salt), which is dried together with pieces of seaweed to increase the salt's mineral content even further. For Japanese home cuisine - which focuses on using ingredients native to Japan - the best match is naturally Japanese salt, a product of the very same environment. However, *tenjitsu-en* is quite expensive, so it's best to use more affordably-manufactured imported solar salts, *ara-jio* (rough salts) for cooking prep stages like boiling in salted water and *shiomomi* (p. 108).

料理の美味しさは塩加減で決まるという定石は世界のどの料理にも共通している。世界にはさまざまな塩があるが、大きくは、汲み上げた海水を製塩した「海塩」と地殻変動などで陸上に閉じ込められた海水の推積層から採掘する「岩塩」に分かれる。

海に囲まれた日本の塩は、ほぼ海塩である。その中でも、塩田 (p.107) で水分を蒸発させたり、釜で煮詰めるなどして物理的に水分を蒸発させただけの「天日塩」は、ミネラルなど海の滋養分がたっぷり残っている。口に含むと旨みや甘みを感じる優しい塩味が特徴なので、料理の味つけには天日塩がおすすめ。なかには藻塩といって海藻を一緒に乾燥させ、よりミネラル分を強めた塩もある。日本の素材を主に用いる日本の家庭料理には、やはり同じ風土で育まれた優しい日本の塩が合う。ただ、天日塩は高価なので、ゆでる、塩もみ (p.108) などの下処理には海外から天日塩を輸入して、良心的な価格で精塩している粗塩を使用するといい。

Shio Uses

Salt has a dehydrating effect due to its strong osmotic pressure. Used as a *shiomomi* for thinly sliced vegetables, it draws moisture out from inside the cells, making the vegetables soft and supple. Not only does this change their firmness and texture, it also makes it easier for other flavors to enter the space between fibers. *Shiomomi* on fish removes the moisture that holds fishy odors, making it delicious when grilled; this is due to the same dehydrating properties of salt. Additionally, salt makes it possible to boil vegetables and retain their innate hues while preventing off-putting color changes. It also has the ability to preserve food, as in *tsukemono* (p. 108), by preventing the growth of bacteria. Further, salt has a contrasting effect on with other flavors: the addition of a small amount of salt can be used as a *kakushi-aji* (p. 109) to bring out sweetness.

There are three different times when salt can be used as a seasoning, each with a different effect: before cooking, during cooking, and after cooking. Salt is used before cooking to draw other seasonings into the ingredients using osmotic pressure, during cooking to add flavor directly, and sparingly after cooking to bring together the flavors of a dish prepared with a lighter flavor profile.

食塩は強い浸透圧の作用による脱水作用を持っている。薄切りにした野菜を塩でもむと、細胞の中から水分が抜け、しんなりする。これは歯ごたえや食感を変えるだけでなく、繊維のすきまに別の味が入りやすくなるという効果も生む。魚に塩をすれば生臭みのある水分が抜け、美味しく魚が焼けるが、これも同様の脱水作用によるものだ。また、野菜を色鮮やかにゆでたり変色を防ぐ作用もあり、漬け物 (p.108) のように塩漬けにすることで雑菌の繁殖を防ぎ、食品を保存する力もある。さらに、味の対比効果といい、塩少々を加えることで他方の甘さを引き立てる隠し味 (p.109) としての使い方もできる。

また、料理における塩のタイミングは、調理前、調理中、調理後と3つあり、それぞれに意味が異なる。調理前の下味の塩は、浸透圧で中まで味を入れるため。調理中の塩はダイレクトな味つけ。そして仕上げの塩は、薄味で調理しておいたものに最後に少量加えて味を調えるためのものだ。

Together with alcohol, *su* (vinegar in Japanese) is one of the oldest seasonings. It's thought that in ancient times collected fruit would naturally ferment to create primitive alcohols, which would then transform into vinegar with bacterial activity. In other words, once you have alcohol, you can create vinegar. Rice in Japan, grapes in France, and malt (barley) in England: these lands' native raw ingredients for alcohol, or even alcohol itself, came to be used for vinegar creation. It's only natural that rice vinegar, full of the gentle sweetness inherent in rice, combines so well with the subdued nuances of Japanese cuisine and directly enlivens its ingredients.

To make rice vinegar as it has been made for centuries: 1) Mix steamed rice with *koji* (p. 110) to create malted rice. 2) Take the malted rice mixture and add yeast, allowing the alcohol fermentation that creates *moromi* (p. 111). 3) Add *tanezu* (a mother of vinegar that generates acetic acid) to the *moromi*. 4) Let the bacteria take in oxygen and the *moromi*'s alcohol, changing the alcohol into vinegar. The surface will be covered with a bacterial film while the vinegar beneath ages. 5) Filter the vinegar and dilute, pasteurize, and bottle as needed. This is the fundamental process in Japanese vinegar manufacturing, and it's important to make sure to check the primary ingredients is rice when you buy Japanese vinegar.

酢は酒と並ぶ最も古い調味料の一つ。太古の昔、蓄えた果物などが自然に発酵して酒の源が生まれ、そこへ菌が働いて酢が誕生したと考えられている。つまり、酢は酒があって初めてできるもの。日本においては米、フランスはぶどう、イギリスではモルト（大麦）と、その土地に根付いた酒の原料、もしくは酒そのものから酢がつくられてきた。米由来の、ふくよかでやわらかな甘みのある米酢が、食材をストレートに生かした、穏やかな日本料理に合うのは必然である。

昔ながらの米酢のつくり方は、①蒸した米に麹菌（p.110）を混ぜて米麹をつくる。②①に酵母を加えてアルコール発酵させて、もろみ（p.111）をつくる。③酢酸菌の入った種酢を加える。④酢酸菌がもろみのアルコール分と空気を取り込み、酒を酢に変える。表面に菌膜がはり、その下で酢が熟成。⑤ろ過し、必要に応じて過水、殺菌、瓶詰め。これが本来の米酢の醸造法で、購入する際には原料が米かを確認することが大切。

Su Uses

Vinegar is rarely used to flavor a dish by itself, and is most often used in conjunction with salt or sugar instead. Even when directly seasoning with vinegar, for example when making *sushi meshi* (p. 102) or *sunomono*, the trick is to combine it with other seasonings to create a balanced tartness. The most important example of this can be found in the salt-vinegar ratio. Vinegar has a mellowing effect on salty flavors, and salt helps soften the tart sharpness of vinegar. Because of this, the ratio of the two is very important.

Vinegar can also be used to dissolve calcium. Simmering sardines in plenty of vinegar dissolves the calcium in their bones, creating a soft, simmered sardine dish that can be eaten bones and all. For acrid, alkaline-tasting vegetables like lotus root or burdock, leaving them exposed to the air after cutting them will cause oxidation and brown discoloring, but since vinegar halts oxidase activity, coating them in vinegar water will keep them white. Vinegar also has a hardening effect on proteins, which is best seen in how we add vinegar to boiling water when making poached eggs. It also strengthens proteins and has the power to kill bacteria, thus preventing decay.

酢は単体で味つけをすることは少なく、塩や砂糖と合わせて使用することが多い。酢の味をダイレクトにつける寿司飯 (p.102) や酢の物においても、ほかの調味料と合わせてほどよく酸味をきかせるのがコツだ。なかでも大切なのは酢と塩の割合。酢には塩味をまろやかにする働きがあり、塩も酢のダイレクトな酸味を和らげる効果がある。

また、酢には、カルシウムを煮溶かす作用がある。鰯をたっぷりの酢で煮ると、骨からカルシウムが溶け出し、骨ごと食べられる柔らかさに煮上がる。れんこんやごぼうなどのアクの強い根菜などは、切ってそのままおくと、空気に触れて酸化し褐色になるが、酢にはこの酸化酵素の働きを食い止める作用があるので、酢水につければ白くなる。たんぱく質を固める作用もあり、酢を加えた湯でポーチドエッグをつくるのはその代表。また、酢にはたんぱく質を強く変化させて菌を殺傷する力もあり、腐敗を防ぐ力もある。

Shoyu

せ

Shoyu (soy sauce in Japanese): the seasoning that symbolizes Japanese food culture. With its mouth-watering aroma and delicate sweetness amidst *umami* (p. 111), soy sauce boasts a balance of flavors unprecedented among the world's seasonings. If we trace back the history of soy sauce, we find its roots in a sauce of ancient China called *hishio*, made from grains steeped in salted water then fermented. Following the introduction of *kinzanji miso* (p. 112) during the *Kamakura* period (1185–1333 AD), soy sauce was perfected and popularized from the *Muromachi* period (1336–1573 AD) onwards. To make soy sauce in the traditional manner: 1) Mix steamed soybeans with roasted wheat in equal proportions. 2) Add *koji* to the mixture. 3) Add saline water, then let ferment and mature to create *moromi*. 4) Once the *moromi* is fully matured, wring the fluid out of it, filter, pasteurize as necessary, and then bottle. Over a lengthy fermentation period ranging from six month to two years, the proteins present in the soybeans are broken down into savory amino acids that impart *umami*, and the sugars of the wheat create the soy sauce's fragrance and sweetness. In addition to the more common *koi-kuchi* (rich) *shoyu*, *usu-kuchi* (light) *shoyu* is made using a shorter fermentation period as well as more wheat and salt. The reason for this is that more soybeans and a longer fermentation period create richer colors in soy sauce.

　日本の食文化を代表する調味料、醤油。食欲をそそる香り、自然の旨み (p.111) をたっぷり含んだ塩味の中の優しい甘みなど、世界的にも類を見ないバランスのとれた調味料だ。醤油の歴史をひもとくと、穀類を塩水に漬けて発酵させた、古代中国の「醤（ひしお）」がルーツだ。鎌倉時代に伝わった金山寺味噌（きんざんじ）(p.112) づくりを経て、室町時代以降に醤油が完成、発展した。伝統的な醤油のつくり方は① 蒸した大豆と炒った小麦を同割で混ぜ合わせる。② ①に麹菌を混ぜる。③ 食塩水を加えて発酵・熟成させ、もろみをつくる。④ 充分に熟成させたもろみを搾り、必要に応じてろ過、火入れして瓶詰め。6か月〜2年に及ぶ長い醸造過程の中で、大豆に含まれるたんぱく質が分解されて、旨みのもとであるアミノ酸になり、小麦の糖分が甘みや香りのもとになる。濃口醤油が一般的だが、淡口醤油は、色づきを抑えるために小麦の割合と塩分を増やして発酵期間を短くしている。なぜなら、大豆が多く、発酵期間が長いほど色が濃くなるためだ。

Shoyu Uses

Though soy sauce may be Japan's unique salt-based seasoning, it is used chiefly for its distinctive aroma and *umami*, not just to add saltiness. Also, because it has a delicate flavor prone to evaporation, for an example *nikujaga* (p. 98), it's best to add soy sauce in the final stages of cooking. By coating ingredients in soy sauce and searing (see *aburu* p. 112) them with a direct flame or on the surface of a naked pan, you'll create a delightful aroma sure to set the mouth to watering. This is owed to the heat-mediated Maillard reaction (p. 113) among the amino acids and sugars present in soy sauce. Actually, the color of soy sauce itself is made possible through the occurrence of the Maillard reaction when sugars and amino acids bond during fermentation. That's why even the color of soy sauce is an important component in its flavor. This can be seen in the complex, mellow browning in simmered dishes made with *koi-kuchi shoyu*. Conversely, while *usu-kuchi shoyu* is indispensable for soups and lightly-colored simmered dishes, it is ultimately used for its saltiness and flavoring capabilities. You'll be able to create a refined *suimono* (p. 113) with careful adjustment of the flavor using salt and a final dash of *usu-kuchi shoyu* at the end for fragrance.

醬油は日本固有の塩味の調味料だが、塩分を補うためだけでなく、主に独特の香りや旨みを補うために加える。しかもその風味は繊細でとびやすいので、料理の終盤に加えるといい。例えば肉じゃが（p.98）でも、煮上がる前に加える。また、素材に醬油を塗って直火で炙ったり（p.112）、鍋肌で焦がすなどすると、より香ばしい食欲をそそる香りが立つ。これは、醬油の中のアミノ酸と糖分が熱によってメイラード反応をおこしたことによるもの。そもそも醬油の色は、発酵中にアミノ酸と糖分が結合してメイラード反応（p.113）をおこすことでできるもの。だから、この色も美味しさの大切な要素なのだ。濃口醬油でこっくりと褐色に煮上げる料理はそれを利用したもの。一方、吸い物（p.113）や淡い色の煮物に欠かせない淡口醬油は、塩味と風味をプラスするために用いる。塩で味を調えておいて、最後に香りづけに淡口醬油を少量落とすことで、洗練された吸い物になる。

Miso

Together with *shoyu*, *miso* is one of the seasonings that symbolize Japanese food culture. Older even than *shoyu*, it came to Japan from ancient China during the *Asuka* period (538–710 AD) as *Kuki*, a sauce of fermented soy beans or grains. *Miso* became widely popular in the *Muromachi* period, when people began to drink it as *miso* soup, for example. As it was once made individually by each household, there is a rich variety of regional *miso*. *Miso* is defined by its raw ingredients: soybeans, *koji*, and salt. *Miso* is subdivided into three general types: if you add rice *koji* to the steamed, crushed soybeans then ferment and age the resulting mixture, you get *kome* (rice)-*miso*; if you add barley *koji* instead, you get *mugi* (barley)-*miso*; if you steep the soy beans themselves in *koji* and ferment that, you get *mame* (soybean)-*miso*. Regionally, the basic *miso* in *Aichi* and central Japan is *mame-miso*; in *Kyushu*, and parts of *Shikoku*, *Chugoku* region, it's *mugi-miso*; and in the other 80% of the country it's *kome-miso*. Based on color, *miso* can be divided into brown *miso* (rice, barley, and some soybean), red *miso* (soybean), and white *miso* (rice). Generally, as a *miso* matures it becomes saltier and takes on a richer, darker color. With a full selection of brown (sweet and salty), red, and white *miso*, you'll be able to accommodate your seasoning to any Japanese dish.

　味噌は醤油と並ぶ、日本の食文化を代表する調味料。その歴史は醤油よりも古く、古代中国から、大豆や穀類を発酵させた古代中国の「豉」が飛鳥時代に伝来したのが起源。室町時代には広く味噌が普及し、味噌汁を飲み始めたとか。かつて、どこの家庭でもつくられていたことから、地方性が豊かで種類も多い。味噌の定義は、原材料が大豆、麹、塩であること。蒸してつぶした大豆に、米麹を加えて発酵熟成させれば米味噌、麦麹を加えれば麦味噌、大豆そのものに麹をつけて発酵させれば豆味噌と3通りに分かれる。地域的には愛知など中部が豆味噌、中国・四国の一部と九州が麦味噌、残る全国8割が米味噌が基本。色で見ると、いわゆる茶色の味噌（米、麦、豆の一部）、赤味噌（豆）、白味噌（米）に分かれる。一般に熟成が長いほど色が濃く、塩分濃度も高くなる。茶色の甘口、辛口、赤、白と揃えれば、どんな日本料理にも対応できる。

Miso Uses

For usage by colors, brown *miso* is used for *miso shiru* (p. 90) and most general *miso* cuisine, saltier red *miso* for *aka-dashi* (red *miso shiru*) and *dengaku* (p. 114), and sweeter white *miso* for *misozuke* and *zōni* (p. 114).

To create truly delicious *miso shiru*, it's important to simmer the ingredients in *dashi* and melt the *miso* into the soup at the very end, immediately turning off the heat afterwards. This is because *miso*'s aromatics evaporate easily, and simmering it for a long time will reduce *umami*, spoil the aroma, and make the texture gritty (see *shitazawari* p. 115). In another vein, the rich and mellow aroma of *miso* is very good at masking the strong odors of any ingredients it's partnered with, which is why powerful-smelling fish like mackerel are often simmered with *miso*.

Additionally, *miso* is the only semi-solid food item among the Japanese seasonings, allowing us to add *mirin*, *sake*, or sugar and make a paste that can be slathered on ingredients for fragrant, delectable grilled dishes. Another typical item of *miso* cuisine is *misozuke*, a type of preservation where vegetables or fish are packed in *miso* paste. *Misozuke* made with fish (see *saikyo-yaki* p. 96) is particularly delicious, and it's an effective method of preserving fish's flavor, which otherwise spoils quickly.

味噌の色による使い分けは、茶色は味噌汁 (p.90) をはじめとする一般的な味噌料理に、辛口の赤は赤だしや田楽 (p.114)、甘口の白は味噌漬けや雑煮などに使う。味噌汁を美味しくつくるには、だしの中で具材を煮、最後に味噌を溶き入れ、すぐに火を止めることが大切。それは、味噌は香りがとびやすいばかりでなく、長く煮ると旨み成分が減り、香りが悪くなり、舌触り (p.115) もざらつくから。一方、味噌には、芳醇な香りで素材の匂いをマスキングする臭み消しの効果も高く、さばのようにくせの強い魚を味噌煮にするのはそのため。

また、味噌は日本固有の調味料の中でも、唯一半固体状の食品で、みりんや酒、砂糖を加えて調味し、食材の上に塗って焼く料理では格別の香ばしさが楽しめる。さらに野菜や魚などを味噌の中に漬け込んで味をつける「味噌漬け」も、味噌の代表的な利用法。なかでも魚の味噌漬けは美味しく、いたみやすい魚を日持ちさせるための手段としても有効だ (p.96)。

Sake

酒

The creation of alcohol emerged naturally and spontaneously in regions all across the world, and though alcohol is prized as a beverage, its ability to help preserve food and enhance the flavor of cuisine was realized very quickly. A variety of alcohols came to be adopted as seasonings in nations everywhere. *Sake* (alcohol in Japanese) may not have a distinctive sweet or salty flavor, but as an example steaming *asari* (short-necked clam) with a shake of *sake* gives them the feel of genuine, unaltered Japanese cuisine. On a similar note, doing the same with wine will give them a European flair, and Shaoxing rice wine will result in a Chinese flavor profile.

In a way, alcohol brings out the feel of a country more clearly than any other seasoning. When compared to the alcohols of other nations, *sake* is characterized by the gentle sweetness inherent to rice, *umami*, and a rich, complex aroma. Contrasted with grape or Shaoxing rice wine, *sake* is notably less acidic. It may not assert its own individual flavor when added to cuisine, but it does lend to a *maroyaka* (p. 115) flavor profile.

　酒は、世界各地で自然発生的につくられ、飲料として珍重されてきたものであるが、いずれの国でも、食材の保存性を高めたり、料理の味を引き立てる効能があるということに早くから気づき、調味料として用いられてきた。いうまでもなく、日本においてはそれが、日本酒である。際立った塩味や甘みがあるわけではないのに、例えばあさりに日本酒をふって蒸せば純和食の風味になる。ちなみに、ワインをふって蒸せば欧風の、紹興酒で蒸せば中華風の味わいになるといった具合だ。

　かように酒は、ある意味ではどんな調味料よりも、その国らしさをはっきりと醸してくれる調味料である。他国の酒と比較した日本酒の特色は、米に由来する優しい甘さと、ふくよかな旨み、奥ゆかしい香りであろう。ワインや紹興酒に比べて酸味が少ないのも特徴だ。だから、日本酒を加えることで、個性を主張するわけではないのに、ふっくらまろやかな (p.115) 味わいに仕上がる。

Sake Uses

As a seasoning, *sake* is used to add flavor and remove unpleasant odors. One of the most common culinary applications of *sake* is in *saka-mushi*, where comparatively light meats like chicken or white-fleshed fish are tossed in *sake* and steamed. The alcohol is heated and evaporated, which acts to steam away any odors lingering on ingredients such as meat and fish. During this process, the alcohol encourages protein solidification and surface hardening, helping to seal in flavor. The flavor remains even as the alcohol evaporates, so when you use sake to steam meat or fish, you end up with a soft, fragrant steamed dish. Going back to our example with clams, we can understand how different alcohols can create a huge variety of differing national flavor profiles: gentle and sweet with *sake*, pleasantly acidic and savory with wine, or rich and complex with Shaoxing rice wine.

Simmering meats with alcohol makes them softer, but this is actually due to the effect of the acids it contains. Also, if using sake in unheated dishes, such as to dilute *tare* (p. 115), you'll need to use the process called *nikiru* by heating it in a pot first to steam off the alcohol content.

　酒を調味料として使う目的の一番は風味づけと臭み消し。なかでも最も一般的なのが「酒蒸し」といって、白身魚や鶏肉など、比較的淡泊な素材に酒をふって蒸す調理法。これは、アルコールが熱によって蒸発するときに、魚や肉などの食材の臭みを一緒にとばしてしまう作用による。この際、アルコールがたんぱく質の凝固を促進して表面を固め、旨みの流出を防ぐ効果もある。アルコール分がとんでも旨みは残るので、しっとりいい香りに蒸し上がるというわけだ。あさりの酒蒸しを例にとると、日本酒ならふっくらした甘み、ワインで蒸せば心地よい酸味と旨み、紹興酒ならコクというように、酒により、あさりの風味が各国風にがらりと変わるのがわかる。

　酒を加えて肉を煮ると柔らかくなるが、これは酒の酸の働きによる。また酒を加熱せずに加える場合は、鍋に入れた酒を温めて火をつけ、アルコール分をとばし「煮切る」ことが必要だ。たれ (p.115) などの濃度をうすめるときなどに使う。

Mirin

みりん

Mirin is a uniquely Japanese seasoning, used to add sweetness and depth of flavor or *teri* (p. 116) to simmered and grilled dishes. When making *mirin*: 1) Rice *koji* is first added to steamed sticky rice. 2) Rice *shochu* (p. 116) is added and the mixture is left to ferment. 3) The *moromi* is matured and then squeezed. Looking at these steps, you can see that even though *mirin* is a seasoning, it's made with the same process as alcohol. At around 12% alcohol, it was prized as a beverage in ancient times. The most compelling explanation for *mirin*'s roots lies with a sweet alcoholic beverage called "*mi-irin*" that came from China during the *Sengoku* period (1467–1573 AD). The multifaceted sweetness, flavor, and aroma that characterize *mirin* come from how the proteins and starch in sticky rice form a complex blend of sugars and amino acids during fermentation.

It's said that *mirin* began to see use as a seasoning midway through the *Edo* period (1603–1868 AD). It came to be combined with *shoyu* to make *kabayaki*'s (p. 116) *tare* and *soba* noodle's *tsuyu* (p. 117), eventually arriving at its status in the present day as one of Japanese cuisine's fundamental seasonings.

みりんは甘みやコクをつけたり、煮物や焼き物に照り (p.116) を出すための調味料で、日本特有のものである。製造工程は、①蒸したもち米に米麹を混ぜる。②米焼酎 (p.116) を加え、発酵させる。③できたもろみを熟成させて絞る。というもので、調味料といえどもその工程は酒そのもの。アルコール度数も12%ほどあり、古い時代には飲料として珍重されてきた。そのルーツは戦国時代に中国から渡来した「密淋」という甘い酒だという説が有力だ。みりん独特の重層的な甘みや風味、香りは、この醸造過程の中で、もち米のでんぷんとたんぱく質が糖分とアミノ酸になって複雑にからみ合うことで生まれる。

調味料として使われるようになったのは江戸時代中期といわれている。みりんと醤油を合わせて蒲焼き (p.116) のたれや、そばのつゆ (p.117) などをつくるようになり、現代に続く日本料理の源が形づくられていった。

Mirin Uses

A uniquely Japanese sweetener, *mirin* allows you to bring a fuller and more elegant sweetness to your dishes when compared with sugar. This is because of the complex variety of sugars - including glucose, dextrose, and oligosaccharides - which are formed from the sticky rice during *mirin*'s fermentation and maturation. When compared with a simple sugar, this combination registers as *maroyaka* sweetness on our tongues. *Mirin* is composed of 50% sugar and 14% alcohol, with the remaining components consisting of amino acids, other extracts, organic acids, aromatic compounds, and so on. As a result, mirin is characterized by a uniquely rich aroma.

The *teri* of Japan's famed *teriyaki* (p. 94) is made possible with *mirin*. Glazing is a phenomenon in which heated sugars gradually become syrup-like, binding to ingredients. Because *mirin* includes such a diverse array of sugars, it creates a far thicker and more beautiful *teri* than sugar would on its own. During this process, the rich amber color that emerges is thanks to the Maillard reaction between the sugars and amino acids in *mirin*. Simply adding sugar to *sake* can't create this kind of effect.

みりんは日本固有の甘味料で、砂糖に比べてふくよかで上品な甘みをつけることができる。それは、みりんが発酵熟成する過程において、もち米から、ブドウ糖、オリゴ糖、グルコースなど多種類の糖が形成されるためで、単一の砂糖に比べて、人間の舌にはまろやかな甘みと感じられるから。みりんの成分は糖分が50%、アルコール分が14%、残りはアミノ酸を中心とするエキス分や有機酸、香り成分などで構成されている。そのため、甘みだけでなく、特有のしっとりとした香りがつくのも特徴。

また、日本を代表する料理の一つである照り焼き (p.94) の「照り」を出すのもみりんの役目。照りとは糖分を加熱したときに、次第にとろりと飴状になって素材にからむ現象をいうが、みりんの場合、何種もの糖分が煮詰まるため、砂糖だけよりもとろりと美しい照りができる。その際、濃い飴色になるのは、みりんの糖類とアミノ酸が結合してメイラード反応をおこすため。日本酒に砂糖を加えて煮詰めてもこうはならない。

Dashi

だし

The supporter of *umami* in *washoku*, *dashi* is fundamental to cookery in Japan. In the broadest sense, the word "*dashi*" refers to a stock where the *umami* of a given ingredient is infused into water through simmering. This can be done with meat, poultry, seafood, and even vegetables. However, when defined more strictly, *dashi* is made by soaking dried ingredients like *konbu*, *katsuobushi*, *iriko* (immature sardines), or *shiitake* mushrooms in water, heating and infusing the water with *umami*. The dominant style of *dashi* nowadays is made by pairing *konbu* with *katsuobushi*, and if you see a reference simply to "*dashi*," it usually refers to this combination. *Dashi* is widely used in a variety of dishes: as *suimono* and *wan-mono* (simmered bowl dishes), as well as *tsuyu* for *udon* and *soba* (noodles), as the stock for simmered dishes, in *ankake* (starch sauce), and elsewhere.

A type of seaweed, *konbu* is dried kelp. *Katsuobushi* is made by filleting skipjack tuna into three pieces, simmering, then smoking and drying. These pieces are then made to repeatedly grow mold and dry out, further removing moisture. For *umami* components, kelp includes quite a lot of glutamate and *katsuobushi* quite a lot of inosinic acid. It's said that combining them creates a synergistic effect which increases overall *umami* by a factor of 10.

「だし」とは和食の旨みを支える、日本料理の根幹である。広義には素材を煮て水に旨みを移したものをいい、肉や魚、貝、野菜などさまざまな素材からとることができる。一方で、狭義の日本料理におけるだしは、昆布、かつお節、いりこ、椎茸などの乾物を水に浸したのちに加熱して、旨みを抽出する方法でとってきた。現在、主流となっているのが、昆布とかつお節を合わせてとる方法で、単に「だし」と表記する場合には多くはこれを指す。吸い物や椀物のつゆになるほか、煮物の煮汁、うどんやそばのつゆ、あんかけなどに広く使われる。

昆布とは、海藻の一種を干したもの。かつお節は、かつおを三枚におろして煮たのち、燻乾してからかびづけして干すことを繰り返し、水分を抜いたもの。昆布は旨み成分の中でもグルタミン酸を多く含み、かつお節はイノシン酸を多く含む。両者を合わせてだしをとることで、旨みは相乗効果で10倍にもなるといわれている。

Dashi Uses

To make dashi, all you need to do is soak *konbu* in water, heat the water, and add *katsuobushi* shavings and filter. Seen from a global perspective, making Japanese *dashi* is remarkably easy and verges on the simplicity of "instant" food. *Umami* has been getting a lot of attention in the world lately, but for the people of Japan, it has been put to good use for a long time as the "sixth" of the five basic Japanese tastes after sweet, salty, sour, spicy, and bitter. This is thanks to *dashi*. Cooking with *dashi* means adding an *umami* flavor profile: *dashi* is thought of as one of the seasonings. Thus, cooking with a rich and savory *dashi* lets you use less of the other seasonings and really bring out the flavor of the ingredients. As a result, you get the benefit of cooking healthy meals that use less salt, sugar, and fat.

　昆布とかつおのだしをとるには、昆布を浸しておいた水を加熱し、削ったかつお節を加えて漉すだけだ。世界的にみれば、日本のだしはインスタントといえるほど簡単にとれることも大きな特徴である。いまでは世界的に注目を集める「旨み」だが、日本人は経験則から、旨みが五味に続く、「第六の味覚」と知っており、さまざまに使いこなしてきた。その要がだしであった。つまり、だしを加えて調理するということは旨みを加えるということで、だしも調味料の一つと考えられる。だから、しっかり旨みが出ただしを用いて料理をつくると、調味料の量が少なくてすみ、素材の味が引き立つ。その結果、塩分、糖分、油脂分の使用量が減り、ヘルシーに料理できるというメリットもある。

Materials and How To Make

First cut a 10 cm (4 in) x 10 cm (4 in) sheet of *konbu* with notches using scissors, then soak in 5 cups (1.2L) of water for one hour. Heat the water on high heat, add about 3 cups of *katsuobushi* shavings once the water begins to bubble, then turn off the heat once the water begins to boil again. Strain the contents once the *katsuobushi* shavings sink. Do not squeeze out the *katsuobushi* shavings at this point. The product of this recipe will keep for two days when refrigerated, and leftovers should be frozen right away.

   In recent years, stores have begun to sell "dried *dashi* stock" as well as "*dashi* packs" which have powdered *katsuobushi* and *konbu* already inside. Feel free to use these for simplicity's sake.

【材料と作り方】
鍋に水6カップ（1.2L）と昆布10cm角（はさみで切り目を入れる）を入れ、1時間浸ける。強火にかけ、沸騰したら、削ったかつお節3カップを加え、再び沸いたら火を止める。かつお節が沈んだら、漉す。このときかつお節は力を入れて絞らないこと。冷蔵庫で2日間保存可能。使用しない分はすぐに冷凍するといい。
　　近年、粉にしたかつお節と昆布をパックに詰めた「だしパック」や、粉末の「だしの素」も販売されているので、簡易にはこれを用いるとよい。

Chapter 2

Condiments

第二章

薬味

Wasabi

山葵

With
Tuna *Sashimi*
まぐろの刺身に添える

An indispensable condiment when eating *sushi,* or *sashimi* (sliced raw seafood), *wasabi* is made by grinding the rhizome of the plant of the same name. *Wasabi* is a member of the brassicaceae family native to Japan that grows on the banks of pristine rivers. The condiment is sometimes called *hon-wasabi* (true *wasabi*) to differentiate it from *seiyo-wasabi* (Western horseradish). Addictively flavorful, *wasabi* comes to the nose with a sharp burn and leaves a fresh and cooling aroma. It has potent antibacterial properties as well, and has been served alongside raw fish since antiquity. Completely different from the spicy capsaicin compound of chilies, the spiciness of *wasabi* comes from mustard oil, a component found in plenty throughout brassicaceae that is generated when *wasabi* is grated down and exposed to the air. This is why the way you choose to grate *wasabi* is important, as a finer grating will result in a more potent aroma and spiciness as well as the emergence of a natural sweetness. Though inferior in aroma and flavor, *wasabi* pastes and *wasabi* powder that dissolves in water are commonly sold in stores and used to substitute for spiciness. However, these preparations do not use *hon-wasabi*, and are mostly made of *seiyo-wasabi*.

　刺身や寿司には欠かせない薬味。わさびは清流に育つ日本原産のアブラナ科の植物で、その地下茎をすりおろして使う。西洋わさびと区別するために、本わさびとも呼ばれる。鼻にツンと抜ける刺激的な辛みと自然な甘み、清涼感のある香りはくせになる美味しさ。抗菌効果も高く、古くから生の魚などに添えられてきた。わさびの辛み成分は、唐辛子類が有するカプサイシンとは全く異なるもので、アブラナ科の植物が多く含む辛子油が、すりおろす過程で空気に触れて生成される成分に由来する。そのため、おろし方が重要で、きめが細かいほど、香り、辛みともに強まり、自然な甘みも引き出される。生に比べて香りと風味は落ちるが、辛さを添える薬味としては代替になる、ペーストや水で溶いて使う粉わさびも多く市販されている。ただ、これらは、日本原産の本わさびではなく、西洋わさびが主原料なものが多い。

Ichimi, Shichimi, Sansho

一味　七味　山椒

On top of Eel *Kabayaki*
うなぎの蒲焼きにふる

Though not great in number, even Japanese cuisine has a few types of powdered seasonings for sprinkling. They stimulate the appetite directly, adding spice, fragrance, and other flavors to dishes. The three representative powdered seasonings in Japan are *ichimi-togarashi*, *shichimi-togarashi*, and *kona-zansho*. "*Ichimi-togarashi*" (lit. "one-flavor chili") refers to cayenne made from dried, powdered chili. Use of chilies took root in Japan after being introduced by Portuguese missionaries in the *Muromachi* period (1336–1573 AD). Using *ichimi-togarashi* as a base, *shichimi-togarashi* (lit. "seven-flavored chili") got its start in the *Edo* period (1603–1868 AD) as a uniquely-Japanese seasoning - and way to feel warm in cold weather - sold at tea houses along shrine and temple approaches. Then in time it was combined with poppy seed, hemp seed, dried ground citrus peel, sesame, *sansho*, *shiso* (perilla), and other ingredients. *Kona-zansho* is made from *sansho* fruit (actually a member of the citrus family) plucked while still green, dried, and turned into a powder. Its unique and refreshing fragrance is most often encountered in *kabayaki* eel dishes.

　種類は多くはないが、日本においても、粉状にしてふりかける香辛料も存在する。それらは料理に辛みや香りなどの風味をつけ、ダイレクトに食欲を刺激する役割を持つ。その代表格が一味唐辛子、七味唐辛子、粉山椒の3つだ。一味唐辛子は室町時代にポルトガル人宣教師が伝え、日本に根付いたといわれる赤唐辛子を乾燥させて粉末にしたもの。江戸時代に参道の茶店で寒さしのぎに売られ始め、次第にけしの実、あさの実、陳皮、ごま、山椒、しそなどを合わせた、日本固有の香辛料「七味唐辛子」として根付いた。粉山椒は、ミカン科の木である山椒の実が熟する前の青いうちに乾燥させて粉末にしたもの。特有の清々しい香りは濃厚なうなぎの蒲焼きとよく合う。

Yuzu-kosho

ゆず胡椒

With
Octopus *Sashimi*
たこの刺身に添える

This paste is characterized by the refreshing aroma of sour *yuzu* citrons and the clear, piercing heat of green chili. *Yuzu-kosho* (or *-gosho*) is made by blending together coarsely crushed green chili and the minced peel of young *yuzu*, adding salt, then *yuzu* juice, and leaving to mature. Until recent decades, this paste was a condiment of considerable local color made at homes across the *Kyushu* region of southern Japan. However, its flavor proved to be universally delicious, and *yuzu-kosho* has now become a popular condiment all across the country. Eaten with hot pot dishes, it also pairs well with *sashimi* made of white-fleshed fish and grilled chicken.

清々しい柚子の香りと青唐辛子の清冽(せいれつ)な辛みが特徴のペースト。製法はみじん切りにした青柚子の皮と粗くすりつぶした青唐辛子に塩を加えてよくすり混ぜ、そこへ柚子果汁を加えてねかせ、熟成させるというものだ。数十年ほど前までは九州各地の家庭でつくられてきた、地方色の強い調味料だったが、その美味しさと汎用性の高さから、いまでは全国区の人気調味料になっている。鍋の薬味にはもちろん、白身魚の刺身につけたり、焼いた鶏肉などに添えて食べるといい。

Sesame

ごま

Grinding
in a mortar
すり鉢でする

A precious crop hailing from Africa but used across the world since ancient times, *goma* (sesame in Japanese) has been important to Japan as well. It has been excavated from *Jomon* period (about 14,000–300 BC) archaeological sites and was already cultivated by the *Nara* period (710–794 AD). Even records passed down to us speak of its use as a raw material for both lamp and cooking oil. After being removed from the pod, *goma* is washed and dried (stopping at this stage results in *arai-goma* [washed sesame]) then roasted. There are many uses for *goma*: it can be sprinkled on dishes as it is, ground in a mortar to create a dressing for *aemono* (dressed salad), or solidified with arrowroot starch to make *goma-dofu*. It spread throughout Japan as an important source of nutrients for *Zen* monks, who were forbidden from eating meat. Though *goma* comes in *shiro* (white)-*goma*, *kuro* (black)-*goma*, and *kin* (gold)-*goma* varieties, the most commonly used in Asia is *kuro-goma*, a type with a potent fragrance.

Sesame seeds themselves are eaten around the world, but as an ingredient cooking sesame oil is used most often in Asia, where it is used to make deep-fried dishes like *tempura* or stir-fried dishes like *kinpira gobo* (simmer-sautéed burdock).

アフリカが原産で、世界中で古代から使用されてきた貴重な穀物。日本でも縄文時代の遺跡から出土し、奈良時代にはすでに栽培され、灯油や食用油の原料として使われてきた記録が残っている。ごまは、さやから取り出して洗って乾燥させ(この状態を洗いごまという)、煎って使用する。料理にそのままふりかけるほか、すり鉢ですってあえ物の衣にしたり、葛粉で固めてごま豆腐にすることも多い。肉食を禁じられた禅僧の大切な栄養源として普及した。ごまには、白ごま、黒ごま、金ごまと種類があるが、香りの強い黒ごまを用いるのはアジアが主である。

世界的に食されているが、食用油としての使用率はアジアが高い。天ぷらなどの揚げ物や、きんぴらごぼうのような炒め煮に用いることが多い。

Kanzuri

かんずり

With *Yakitori*
焼き鳥に添える

Hailing from Japan's snowy northern coast, *kanzuri* is a paste seasoning made from red chili. Its method of preparation run by one and only maker hasn't changed in hundreds of years: the rich, fleshy red chili of *Myoko, Niigata* prefecture are salt-pickled then planted out in the snow for three days and nights to remove salt and bitterness. The fibers of the chilies soften, and they're then mixed in with salt, *koji*, and *yuzu* and fermented for three or more years in a particularly time-intensive production. Most often eaten with hot pots, *kanzuri* also tastes delicious as a condiment for *yakitori* (skewer-grilled chicken) and *kara-age* (deep-fried chicken), and it makes an excellent addition to any dish in which you want to evoke a rich, fatty flavor.

　雪国で生まれた赤唐辛子のペースト状の調味料。その歴史は古く、数百年来変わらない製法を、ただ一軒の製造元が守り続けている。まず、塩漬けにした新潟・妙高産の肉厚の赤唐辛子を雪の上に蒔いて3昼夜おき、アクと塩分を抜く。繊維が柔らかくなった赤唐辛子に、麹、柚子、塩を加え、3年以上発酵熟成させる、という手間隙かけたもの。鍋の薬味に使うのが一般的だが、熟成による、心地よい酸味が、濃厚な油脂分を感じさせる料理にも合い、焼き鳥や唐揚げにつけても美味しい。

Umeboshi

梅干し

In *Onigiri*
おにぎりに入れる

An indispensable foodstuff for *bento* lunchboxes and *onigiri* (rice ball), *umeboshi* is made by salt-pickling then sun-drying the fruit of the *ume*, also known as the Japanese apricot. The *ume* is originally from China, and *umeboshi* was first used medicinally as a pulpy byproduct of the process to create *ume* vinegar. Later, *umeboshi* came to Japan, and from the *Sengoku* period (1467–1573 AD) onward it saw regular use. For example, it was popular as a preserved food and to prevent food poisoning, an effect realized by its potent citric acid concentration. *Umeboshi* has become an important and distinctly Japanese constituent element of flavor; its unique salty sourness not only goes well with white rice but is also used in a broad range of cuisine like dressed salad, simmered dishes, and grilled dishes. Until *shoyu* spread across the country in the mid-*Edo* period (18th century AD), *umeboshi* was even simmered in *sake* to create a salty liquid seasoning called *irizake*.

　梅の実を塩漬けにしたのち、天日干ししたもので、お弁当やおにぎりには欠かせない食材。梅は中国が原産で、梅酢をとった副産物の果肉を薬用に用いたのが梅干しの起源。その後日本に伝わり、戦国時代以来保存食として重用され、食中毒の予防などにも盛んに使われた。その効能は梅の持つ強いクエン酸によるもの。特有の"酸っぱくてしょっぱい"味わいは、おにぎりやごはんの友以外にも、あえ物、煮物、焼き物などさまざまな料理に使われ、日本的な風味を形成する大切な要素の一つとなっている。醤油が普及する江戸時代半ばまでは、日本酒で梅干しを煮た液体を「煎り酒」として、塩味をつける調味料に用いた。

Chapter 3

Sauces

第三章

つゆとたれ

Soba-tsuyu

そばっゆ

Soba-tsuyu is dipping *tsuyu* sauce served in *soba* restaurants which uses *kaeshi* including sugar, *shoyu*, and *mirin* diluted with *dashi*. Restaurants add more *dashi* for *kake soba*, a hot soupy style of *soba*. This recipe is for home cooking. Feel free to use one of the many widely-sold instant *soba tsuyu* products.

Ingredients————————Serves 3-4

A
- 5/6 (200ml) cup water
- 3 Tbsp + 1 tsp (50ml) *sake*
- 1 cup *katsuobushi*
1 tsp *mirin*
4 Tbsb *shoyu*

1　In a small saucepan, boil A for 5-6 minutes.

2　Add *mirin* and stir. Bring to a boil again. Turn off heat, pour in *shoyu* and stir. Remove from heat and cool.

3　Pour through a strainer to remove *katsuobushi*. After straining, *soba-tsuyu* should be clear.

Notes:
- *Soba-tsuyu* can be used immediately or kept in the refrigerator for 1 week.

そばつゆ

そばを食べるためのつゆ。そば屋では醤油、砂糖、みりんを合わせた「かえし」をだしで割って、そばつゆとして供する。つゆをたっぷりかけるかけそばでは、希釈するだしの割合を増やして使用する。ここでは家庭で作りやすい簡易版のそばつゆを紹介する。既成のそばつゆも多く販売されているので利用するのもいい。

材料（3〜4人分）
A
- 水…1カップ
- 酒…1/4カップ
- かつお節…1カップ
みりん…小さじ1
醤油…大さじ4

1　小鍋にAを入れて沸かし、弱めの中火にして5〜6分煮る。

2　1にみりんを加えて再度沸かし、火を止め、醤油を加え、混ぜる。

3　人肌に冷めたら漉す。

作り方のコツ
冷蔵庫で1週間は保存できる。

Zaru soba

Soba means buckwheat in Japanese, and these long, thin noodles are made from buckwheat flour. *Zaru soba* is served cold with *nori*, and dipped in a *soba choko* (small cup) of *soba-tsuyu*.

Ingredients ──────── Serves 4

200 g (7 oz) *soba* noodles
3-4 sheets *nori* (dried seaweed)
1/4 *naganegi* leek
5/6 cup (200ml) *soba-tsuyu*

Condiments
Wasabi

1. Cut *nori* into strips, slice *naganegi* thinly, and grind *wasabi*.

2. Boil water in a large saucepan on high heat. Put *soba* noodles in the pot and boil. Stir occasionally. Drain using a strainer or basket. Quickly rinse noodles with cold water to stop the cooking process.

3. Place noodles on a bamboo basket. Sprinkle *nori* strips on top of *soba* noodles. Pour *soba-tsuyu* into small cup. To eat, put *naganegi* and *wasabi* into the *soba-tsuyu* and dip *soba* noodles.

Notes:
- There are many kinds of *soba* products; follow the instructions on the product package regarding cooking times.
- At *soba* restaurants, *soba-yu* the hot water that the *soba* was boiled in will be served at the end of the meal. Add *soba-yu* to your remaining *soba-tsuyu* in a cup and drink it.

ざるそば

材料 (4人分)
そば…200g
のり…3〜4枚
長ねぎ…¼ 本
そばつゆ…1 カップ

薬味
わさび

作り方
1 のりは細く切り、長ねぎを小口から薄切りにする。わさびはすりおろす。

2 大きな鍋に湯を沸かし、そばを入れて時々混ぜながらゆでてざるに上げ、冷えるまで冷水ですすぐ。

3 竹ざるなどにそばを盛り、のりをふり、そばつゆと長ねぎ、わさびを添える。

作り方のコツ
そばには乾麺、生麺など多種あり、ゆで時間は商品パッケージの記載を参照。

そば屋で最後に供されるそば湯は、適宜残ったそばつゆに足して味わう。

Kizami udon

Udon noodles are made from wheat flour. This hot soup is clear in the Western style, and pale in color. *Abura-age* is a thin, deep-fried *tofu* that adds texture and taste.

Ingredients————————Serves 4

300 g (10 oz) *udon* noodles
2 sheets of *abura-age* (thin, deep-fried *tofu*)
4 *aonegi* (spring onions)
1/3 cup + 4 tsp (100ml) *soba-tsuyu*
About 4 cups *dashi* (1L)
1 Tbsp salt

Condiments

Ichimi, *shichimi* and *sansho* peppers, or
yuzu-kosho

1 Boil water in a small pot, and then add
abura-age for 2-3 minutes to remove
the oil. Drain the hot water and rinse
with cold water. Once cool, squeeze
with both hands to remove water. Slice
abura-age to 1 cm (0.4 in) wide and
aonegi to 5 cm (2 in) long.

2 Boil water in a large saucepan. Add
udon noodles to boil.

3 Boil *dashi* in another pot. Add *soba-
tsuyu* and *abura-age* and boil quickly.
Add salt and #2 *udon* noodles, then
cook 1-2 minutes. Turn off heat and
add *aonegi*. To eat, place *udon* in
individual bowls and add soup. Use
condiments as you like.

Notes:
- There are many kinds of *udon* products;
follow the instructions on the product package
regarding cooking times.

きざみうどん

材料（4人分）
うどん…300ｇ
油揚げ…2枚
青ねぎ…4本
そばつゆ…½カップ
だし…約5カップ
塩…大さじ1

薬味
一味唐辛子　七味唐辛子、
粉山椒、ゆず胡椒

作り方
1 小鍋に湯を沸かし、油揚げ
を2〜3分ゆでてざるに取る。
流水でさっと洗って水けを絞り、
油抜きし、1cm幅に切る。青ね
ぎは5cm長さに切る。

2 大きな鍋に湯を沸かし、うど
んをゆでる。

3 別の鍋にだしを沸かし、そば
つゆと油揚げを入れてさっと煮
る。塩で調味し、2のうどんを
加えて1〜2分煮る。火を止め
て青ねぎを加え、丼に盛り、好
みの薬味を添える。

作り方のコツ
うどんには乾麺、ゆで麺、生麺
など多種あり、ゆで時間は商
品パッケージの記載を参照。

Ponzu

ぽんず

This tangy *tare* sauce varies by region according to the citrus grown locally. *Ponzu* basically consists of juice squeezed from citrus fruits, *shoyu*, and *su*, additional ginger, *negi*, *konbu*, and *katsuobushi* for its extra *umami*. It can be used as a dipping sauce for hot pots, a marinade for *sashimi* (raw fish), or a dressing for vegetable salads or fried foods. Feel free to use instant *ponzu* products as great substitutes for homemade.

Ingredients ——————— Serves 3-4

A
- 1/3 cup + 4 tsp (100ml) *dashi*
- 3 Tbsp *sake*

3 Tbsp + 1 tsp (50ml) *shoyu*

B
- 3 Tbsp + 1 tsp (50ml) squeezed citrus juice
- 2 Tbsp vinegar

1 Bring A to a boil in a saucepan over medium heat and boil for 2-3 minutes. Turn off heat and add *shoyu*.

2 Add B, stir, and let cool. Pour into a jar and keep covered in the refrigerator. After 1 week, the *ponzu* is ready to use.

Notes:

- *Yuzu*, *kabosu*, *sudachi*, *daidai* or lemon citrus fruits can all be used. Mix a few kinds to deepen its flavor.
- *Ponzu* can be kept in the refrigerator for an additional 2 weeks.

ポン酢

日本各地の柑橘類の搾り汁に醤油や酢などを加えたたれ。ねぎやしょうがなどの香味野菜や、昆布、かつお節などの旨みを加えることもある。鍋物のつけだれとして使うのが一般的だが、サラダのドレッシングや刺身のつけだれ、また揚げ物にかけても美味と、汎用性が高い合わせ調味料だ。市販のぽん酢を利用するのもいい。

材料（3〜4人分）
A
- だし…½カップ
- 酒…大さじ3
醤油…¼カップ
B
- 柑橘類の搾り汁…¼カップ
- 米酢…大さじ2

作り方

1 小鍋にAを入れ、2〜3分煮立てて火を止め、醤油を加える。

2 Bを加えて冷ます。保存容器などに移し、冷蔵庫で1週間ほどおいて味がなれてから使用する。

作り方のコツ

柑橘類はゆず、かぼす、すだち、橙、レモンなどが使用できる。2〜3種を混ぜると味に深みが出る。

さらに冷蔵庫で2週間は保存できる。

65

Aemono with *Wakame* and Cucumber

Aemono is a cold side dish of tossed vegetables with tangy dressing such as *ponzu*. It is a Japanese style salad which easily can be arranged with other ingredients as you may like.

Ingredients————————Serves 4

2 cucumbers
2 tsp salt
1/5 cup *wakame* (dried seaweed)
3 Tbsp *ponzu*

Condiments

1 Tbsp roasted white *goma* (sesame)

1 Slice cucumbers in half lengthwise and remove seeds with a small spoon. Slice the cucumber very thinly on a diagonal. Place in a bowl and sprinkle with salt. Let sit for 10 minutes. Squeeze to remove water.

2 Soak *wakame* in cold water and drain. If needed, cut *wakame* into 2 cm (0.8 in) strips.

3 Place in individual bowls, add cucumbers and *wakame*, then drizzle with *ponzu*. Sprinkle sesame seeds on top.

Notes:

- Do not soak the seaweed for too long or it will lose its texture.

わかめときゅうりの あえ物

材料（4人分）
きゅうり…2本
塩…小さじ2
わかめ（乾燥）…$\frac{1}{4}$カップ
ポン酢…大さじ3

薬味
白煎りごま…大さじ1

作り方
1 きゅうりは縦半分に切ってスプーンで種を取り、斜め薄切りにする。塩をまぶして10分おき、水けを絞る。

2 わかめは水でもどし、水けをきって2cm長さに切る。

3 器にきゅうりとわかめを盛り、ポン酢をかけ、ごまを散らす。

作り方のコツ
わかめは戻し過ぎると歯ごたえがなくなるので注意。

Tara Chiri

Tara Chiri is a cod hot pot cooked in a *donabe* (Japanese clay pot) over a portable burner at the table with family and friends. It pairs well with warm *sake*.

Ingredients————————Serves 4

2 fresh *tara* (cod) fillets
1 block *momen* (firm) tofu
4 bunch *shungiku* (chrysanthemum stems with leaves)
A
┌ **1 2/3 cups (400ml) water**
└ **5 cm (2 in) x 5 cm *konbu***
3 Tbsp + 1 tsp *sake*
About 1/4 cup (60ml) *ponzu*

Condiments

Ichimi* pepper or *yuzu-kosho

1 Wipe cod skin with a paper towel against the scale grain and cut into 4 cm (1.5 in) pieces. Wipe *tofu* with a paper towel and cut into 4 cubes. Cut off the hard bottom of *shungiku* stems.

2 Put A into a small clay pot. Leave to infuse for 30 minutes, then bring to a boil over medium heat. After the water boils, add *sake*. Add the cod to the pot and cook until the cod changes to a white color (about 2-3 minutes).

3 Add *tofu* once the cod is cooked, then add *shungiku*. Place in individual bowls at the table. Eat by dipping ingredients in *ponzu* and sprinkling spices on top.

Notes:
- Chinese cabbage or watercress can also be added.

たらちり

材料 (4人分)
たら切り身…2切れ
木綿豆腐…1丁
春菊…4本
A
┌水…2カップ
└昆布 (5cm角)…1枚
酒…1/4カップ
ポン酢…約1/3カップ

薬味
一味唐辛子、ゆず胡椒

作り方
1 たらは皮のぬめりをキッチンペーパーで拭き取り、4cm角に切る。豆腐はキッチンペーパーで包んで軽く水けをきり、4等分に切る。春菊は軸のかたい部分は切り落とす。

2 小ぶりの土鍋にAを入れて30分おいて火にかける。沸いたら酒を加え、たらを入れる。

3 たらに火が通ったら豆腐を入れ、最後に春菊を加える。ポン酢をつけ、好みの薬味を添えて食べる。

作り方のコツ
白菜、芹やクレソンなどを加えてもいい。

Goma-dare

ごまだれ

This is a sesame dipping *tare* sauce used mainly for *shabu shabu*, poured over cold *tofu*, or used as a dressing for boiled or fresh vegetables. It consists of sesame paste with sugar, vinegar and *shoyu* diluted with *dashi*. In addition to using *neri goma* (sesame paste) products, *suri goma* (ground sesame) can also be used to give extra texture.

Ingredients————————Serves 3-4

3 Tbsp + 1 tsp *shiro neri goma* (white sesame paste)

1 tsp sugar

1 Tbsp *shoyu*

1 Tbsp vinegar

1-2 Tbsp ground *shiro iri goma* (roasted white sesame)

3 Tbsp + 1 tsp *dashi*

Stir all seasonings together in a bowl and pour in *dashi* to combine. Mix well till it becomes smooth and creamy.

Notes:

- Can keep in the refrigerator for up to 1 week. Mix well before using, as oil and sesame paste will not separate.

- If available, *usukuchi-shoyu* is preferable.

ごまだれ

練りごまに、砂糖、醤油、酢を加えて混ぜ、だしなどで希釈したつけだれ。最も一般的な用途は牛肉や豚肉などのしゃぶしゃぶのたれだが、豆腐にかけたり、野菜のあえ物などに用いることも多い。市販の練りごまだけでなく、煎りごまをすったものを加えて食感を楽しむのもいい。

材料（3〜4人分）
白練りごま…1/4カップ
砂糖…小さじ1
醤油…大さじ1
酢…大さじ1
白煎りごまをすったもの
…大さじ1〜2
だし…1/4カップ

作り方
ボウルにねりごまを入れ、調味料とすりごまを加えてよく混ぜ、だしを少しずつ加えてなめらかになるまでのばしていく。

作り方のコツ
冷蔵庫で1週間は保存できる。使うときに、よく混ぜること。

醤油は淡口醤油が手に入ればよりよい。

Goma-ae with Spinach

Goma-ae is a type of *aemono* made using *goma-dare*.
It is also a cold side dish. *Kuro goma* (black sesame) is used
where available to add a strong flavor.

Ingredients————————Serves 4

1 bunch spinach
1 Tbsp salt
About 1/4 cup (60ml) *goma-dare*

Condiments

1 Tbsp ground *shiro iri goma* (roasted white sesame)

1 Boil a pot of water with salt on high heat. Quickly submerge the bunch of spinach from its bottom into the pot of boiling water for about 1-2 minutes until spinach changes to a bright green. Drain water, and plunge spinach into a bowl of cold water to stop the cooking process. Once cool, squeeze spinach upside-down with your hands to remove excess water.

2 Cut spinach into 5 cm (2 in) lengths. Place spinach in a serving bowl. Drizzle *goma-dare* over spinach and sprinkle with ground *goma*. Spinach and *goma-dare* can be mixed after serving.

Notes:
- *Shoyu* can be added to *goma-dare* if you prefer a saltier taste, or vinegar can be added to *goma-dare* to increase depth of flavor.

ほうれん草のごまあえ

材料（4人分）
ほうれん草…1束
塩…大さじ1
ごまだれ…約⅓カップ

薬味
白煎りごま…大さじ1

作り方
1 沸騰した湯に塩を加え、ほうれん草を軸側から入れて色が変わるまで1〜2分ゆでる。冷水にさらし、冷たくなったら、葉を下にして水けを絞る。

2 ほうれん草は5cm長さに切り、器に盛り、ごまだれをかけ、白ごまをふる。

作り方のコツ
ごまだれに、醤油を足して塩加減を調整したり、酢を加えて深味を増したりできる。

Shabu Shabu

Shabu shabu is an easily-prepared Japanese hot pot.
This is a perfect main course for home parties with close friends
and family, as everyone takes part in cooking at the table.

Ingredients ———————— Serves 4

500 g (1lb) thinly-sliced beef thigh
5 long leaves *hakusai* (Chinese cabbage)
4 *shiitake* mushrooms
1 *naganegi* leek
1 package *kudzukiri* (noodle-like products made from roots of the *kudzu* vegetable)
A
⌐ About 4 cups (1L) water
└ 5/6 cup (200ml) *sake*
5/6 cup (200ml) *goma-dare*
5/6 cup (200ml) *ponzu*
1/3 cup sliced *asatsuki* (scallion)

Condiments

Ichimi pepper or *kanzuri*

1   Cut *hakusai* into bite-size strips.
Cut off *shiitake* stems and make an incision in the heads to make a cross shape. Slice *naganegi* in half lengthwise and remove the hard yellow core, then cut into 5 cm (2 in) lengths.

2   Arrange #1, *kudzukiri*, and beef separately on a serving plate.
Pour each of *ponzu* and *goma-dare* into individual bowls for dipping.
Place *asatsuki* on top of *goma-dare*.

3   Pour A into a big pot and bring to a boil on medium heat on top of a gas burner at the table. Once the meat gives the broth a tasty flavor, add vegetables and *kudzukiri* cook for 2-3 minutes.

4   Remove to a plate and dip in *ponzu* or *goma-dare* with condiments as you like. Repeat this process.

Notes:

- Use a spoon to skim the scum off the water occasionally.
- At the end of the meal, add *udon* to the pot and boil for 2-3 minutes.

しゃぶしゃぶ

材料 (4人分)
牛肉 (しゃぶしゃぶ用)
…500g
白菜…5枚
椎茸…4枚
長ねぎ…1本
葛きり…1袋
A
⌐ 水…約5カップ
└ 酒…1カップ
ごまだれ…1カップ
ポン酢…1カップ
あさつき(小口切り)…½カップ

薬味
一味唐辛子、かんずり

作り方

1 白菜は食べやすい大きさに切る。椎茸は軸を除き、かさに十文字の切り込みを入れる。長ねぎは縦半分に切り、芯を除き、5cm長さに切る。

2 大皿に1と葛きり、牛肉を盛り合わせる。たれを用意する。

3 大きめの鍋にAを沸かし、牛薄切り肉をしゃぶしゃぶし、肉のだしが出たら、野菜や葛きりも加えて火を通す。

4 あさつきを加えたごまだれとポン酢に、好みでつけながら食べる。薬味は好みで一味唐辛子やかんずりを添える。

作り方のコツ
途中、アクはこまめに取ること。

締めにゆでたうどんを加えるのもいい。

Warishita

わりした

Warishita is mainly used as *sukiyaki* sauce. Basically, it is a *shoyu*-based sauce consisting of *mirin*, sugar, and *sake* or *dashi*. It literally means "dividing sauce," and tastes strongly enough to give flavor when used in cooking.

Ingredients————————Serves 3- 4

5/6 cup (200ml) *shoyu*
3 Tbsp + 1 tsp *sake*
3 Tbsp + 1 tsp water
3 Tbsp sugar

Add all ingredients to a small saucepan on medium heat and stir to combine. Bring to a boil and turn off heat once sugar has melted.

Notes:

- Use immediately or keep covered in a jar in the refrigerator for up to 1 week.

割り下

「割り下」とは、醤油に、みりん、砂糖、酒、またはだしを加えて煮立てた汁のことで、すき焼きのたれを指していうことが多い。本来は「割り下地」といい、味つけのもととなる醤油（下地）を他の調味料やだし汁で割った味の濃い（だしが少なく、調味料が多い）ものを指す。

材料（3〜4人分）
醤油…½カップ
酒…¼カップ
水…¼カップ
砂糖…大さじ3

作り方
小鍋にすべての材料を入れ、砂糖が溶けるまでさっと煮る。

作り方のコツ
冷蔵庫で1週間は保存できる。

Oyakodon

This easy, home-style recipe is usually served for lunch. Chicken and egg are cooked with *warishita* and then placed over a *donburi* (bowl) of *gohan* (cooked rice).

Ingredients ——————————— Serves 4

2 pieces, about 500g (1lb) chicken thigh
1 large white onion
A
- **1 2/3 cups (400ml) *warishita***
- **1/3 cup + 4 tsp (100ml) water**

B
- **2 tsp *katakuriko* (potato starch)**
- **1 Tbsp water**

8 eggs
4 individual bowls of *gohan* (cooked rice)
8 sheets of *nori* (dried seaweed)

Condiments

***Sansho*, *shichimi*, and *ichimi* pepper**

1. Remove the chicken skin, cut off the fat, and remove the tendons and gristle. Cut the chicken into bite-sized pieces. Peel onion skin, cut in half, and slice onion into strips very thinly.

2. Put A in a pan on medium heat. Once it simmers, add chicken and cook for about 2-3 minutes. Add onion and cook for 1 minute more. Stir occasionally.

3. Stir together B in a small bowl. Add B to #2 pan to thicken the sauce and stir to dissolve. Remove from heat and set aside.

4. Scoop *gohan* (see the instruction p.92) into 4 individual bowls. Sprinkle the 2 sheets of hand-cut *nori* on top.

5. Put 1/4 of #3 into a small saucepan and reheat on medium heat. Crack eggs into a bowl and mix slightly. Drizzle the 1/4 of egg into the pan and stir slowly to cook and combine. After 30 seconds, turn off the heat and cover. Leave covered for 2-3 minutes to half-cook eggs.

6. Place #5 on top of #4. Sprinkle condiments on top. Repeat the cooking process 3 more times for each bowl.

親子丼

材料（4人分）
鶏もも肉…2枚（約500g）
玉ねぎ…大1個
A
- 割り下…2カップ
- 水…½カップ

B
- 片栗粉…小さじ2
- 水…大さじ1

卵…8個
ごはん…多めの4膳
のり…8枚

薬味

粉山椒、七味唐辛子、一味唐辛子

作り方
1 鶏もも肉は皮と脂を除き、ひと口大のそぎ切りにする。玉ねぎは縦半分に切り、薄切りにする。

2 鍋にAを入れて中火にかけ、沸いたら鶏肉を加えて2～3分煮る。続いて玉ねぎを入れ、1分煮る。

3 2にBを加え、とろみがついてくるまで混ぜ、火からおろす。

4 それぞれの丼にごはん（炊き方p.92）を盛り、2枚分のちぎったのりをのせる。

5 小さいフライパンなどに3の1/4量を入れて中火にかけ、煮立ってきたら溶いた卵の1/4量を少しずつ流し入れる。30秒ほどで火を止め、ふたをして2～3分蒸らし、半熟にする。

6 5を4のごはんにすべらせるようにのせ、好みの薬味をふる。同様の作業を3回繰り返して4人分を仕上げる。

Sukiyaki

Sukiyaki is one of the most popular Japanese hot pot dishes.
It is a perfect party treat served on special occasions
during holiday seasons. *Sukiyaki* can be cooked in the kitchen
using a large frying pan.

Ingredients—————————————Serves 4

1 500 g (1!b) thinly-sliced beef loin
1 bag of *shirataki* (thinly-sliced *konnyaku*)
1 tsp salt
1 block *yaki dofu* (pre-grilled *tofu*)
1 *naganegi* leek
1 bunch *shungiku* (chrysanthemum stems with leaves)
4 *shiitake* mushrooms
1 block of beef fat or 1 Tbsp vegetable oil
5/6 cup (200ml) *warishita*
4 eggs

1 Transfer *shirataki* to a bowl, remove water, add salt and gently rub with your hands. Place in a pot of water and boil, then drain the water. Cool and then cut into half length.

2 Wrap *tofu* in a paper towel for a while to remove moisture. Then slice *tofu* in 2 cm (0.8 in) widths. Cut *naganegi* on the diagonal to about 5 cm (2 in) in length. Cut off the hard bottoms of the *shungiku*. Cut off the stems of the *shiitake* and make incisions in the tops in cross shapes.

3 On a large, flat serving platter, place #1, 2, and beef into separate piles.

4 Heat the iron *sukiyaki* pan on medium heat on top of a gas burner at the table. Once heated, add beef fat cubes or oil and quickly spread around to coat the pan. Quickly pan-fry both sides of beef until it changes color. Add the *shirataki* and *tofu* (do not stir the *shirataki* with beef). Pour in a half cup of *warishita* and cook ingredients for 1-2 minutes. Add the *naganegi*, *shiitake*, and *shungiku* briefly.

5 Crack eggs into individual bowls and whisk with chopsticks. Remove cooked ingredients from pan then dip into the raw egg and eat. Repeat this process by cooking in the pan and adding *warishita* each time.

Notes:
- Watercress can be used instead of *shungiku*.
- In western Japan, people use sugar and *shoyu* instead of *warishita*.

すき焼き

材料（4人分）
牛ロース肉（すき焼き用）…500g
しらたき…1袋
塩…小さじ1
焼き豆腐…1丁
長ねぎ…1本
春菊…1わ
椎茸…4個
牛脂または植物油…適宜
割り下…1カップ
卵…4個

作り方
1 しらたきの水けをきり、塩を加えてもみ、水をたっぷり加えてゆでる。ざるに上げ、半分の長さに切る。

2 焼き豆腐はキッチンペーパーで包んで軽く水けをきり、2cm厚さに切る。長ねぎは5cm長さの斜めに切り、春菊は軸を切り落とす。椎茸は軸を切り、かさに十文字に切り目を入れる。

3 大皿に1、2、牛ロース肉を盛り付ける。

4 鉄鍋を中火で熱し、牛脂を溶かし、牛肉を加えて両面を焼き、牛肉から離れた所にしらたきを入れ、豆腐を盛る。割り下の半量を注ぎ、1〜2分でふつふつしてきたらねぎと椎茸を加えて少し煮る。最後に春菊を加えてさっと火を通す。

5 小鉢に卵を割りほぐし、煮えた具を取り、卵をつけて食べる。煮詰まってきたら適宜、割り下を足す。

作り方のコツ
春菊のかわりに、芹やクレソンなどを加えてもいい。

関西のすき焼きは割り下を作らずに、直接、砂糖や醤油などの調味料を加えて作ることも多い。

Ten-tsuyu

天つゆ

Ten-tsuyu is *tempura* dipping *tsuyu* sauce consisting of *dashi*, *shoyu*, and *mirin*. This sauce is one of the fundamental seasoning of Japanese food, and is easily arranged by *dashi* dilution ratios from thicker to lighter. Add *usukuchi-shoyu* or *koikuchi-shoyu* to finish.

Ingredients——————— Serves 3-4

5/6 cup (200ml) *dashi*
3 Tbsp *mirin*
2 Tbsp *shoyu*

Boil *dashi* in a saucepan and then add *mirin*. Stir and boil for another 30 seconds. Add *shoyu* and then turn off the heat. Cool to room temperature.

Notes:
- Can be kept in the refrigerator for 3-4 days.
- If available, *usukuchi-shoyu* is preferable.

天つゆ

天ぷらを食べるためのつゆ。だし、醤油、みりんを合わせてひと煮立ちさせたもの。この組み合わせは、日本料理の味つけの基本となるもので、薄味の煮物から濃い味のつけだれまで、だしの希釈割合を変えるだけで、さまざまに応用がきく。また好みに応じて、濃口と淡口の醤油を使い分ける。

材料（3～4人分）
だし…1カップ
みりん…大さじ3
醤油…大さじ2

作り方
小鍋にだしを沸かし、みりんを加えてさらに30秒煮て、醤油を加えて火を止め、室温に冷ます。

作り方のコツ
冷蔵庫で3～4日保存できる。

醤油は淡口醤油が手に入れば、使い分けるとよい。

Agedashi Dofu

This is a typical *izakaya* (tavern) menu item as a perfect hot appetizer. "*Agedashi*" means deep-fried food eaten with *dashi* broth.

Use tools gently when handling *tofu*, as it can break easily.

Ingredients————————Serves 4

1 package of *momen* (firm) *tofu*
1 egg white
3 Tbsp + 1 tsp *katakuriko* (potato starch)
Vegetable oil for frying
5/6 cup (200ml) *ten-tsuyu*
1 tsp grated ginger

1 Remove water from *tofu* by wrapping
  2 thick paper towels around the *tofu*
  block. Place in between 2 cutting
  boards horizontally and slant the *tofu* so
  that water runs off. Leave for 30 minutes.
  Unwrap the *tofu* and slice into 4 cubes.

2 Whisk the egg white until it becomes
  foamy. Quickly dip *tofu* in the egg
  white and gently coat it on all sides by
  sprinkling with *katakuriko*.

3 Heat oil on medium heat in a pan until
  it is 150°C (300°F). The oil is ready if
  bubbles rise to the surface when you
  put a skewer in the center. Using a flat
  spatula to pick up #2 *tofu* and then
  slide it into the oil. Fry for 3-4 minutes
  until lightly browned and crispy. Remove
  and place on paper towel.

4 Place *tofu* in individual serving bowls.
  Pour a small amount of warm *ten-tsuyu*
  over the *tofu*. Top with grated ginger.

揚げ出し豆腐

材料（4人分）
木綿豆腐…1丁
卵白…1個分
片栗粉…½カップ
揚げ油…適宜
天つゆ…1カップ
おろししょうが…小さじ1

作り方

1 豆腐は厚手のキッチンペー
パー2枚で包み、まな板に水
平にはさんで30分おく。水き
りして、4等分する。

2 よく溶いた卵白にすばやくく
ぐらせ、片栗粉を全体にまぶし
つける。

3 揚げ油を150℃に熱する。
菜箸を油の中に入れたときに、
細かい気泡が上がるくらいなら
適温。2の豆腐を油に入れ、
周囲がカリッとするまで3〜4
分揚げ、キッチンペーパーの
上に取り、油をきる。

4 器に盛り、温めた天つゆを
注ぎ、おろししょうがをのせる。

Tempura

Tempura is deep-fried seafood and vegetables. The most important keys to succeeding in home-cooking *tempura* are the timing and temperature used in frying. The formula of the oil and the flour used for batter can encompass a wide variety of types when you eat at *tempura* restaurants.

Ingredients————————Serves 4

8 fresh shrimp (about 10cm / 4in long)
8 slices *satsuma-imo* (Japanese sweet potatoes)
8 leaves green *shiso* (perillas)
Batter
A
┌ **1 egg**
└ **5/6 cup (200ml) cold water**
B
┌ **1/3 cup + 4 tsp (100ml) soft flour**
└ **3 Tbsp + 1 tsp *katakuriko* (potato starch)**
Vegetable oil for frying
5/6 cup (200ml) *ten-tsuyu*
1/3 cup grated *daikon* (Japanese radish)
1 Tbsp grated ginger

1 Prepare batter. Mix A well in a bowl, and put B in another bowl. Keep them cold in a refrigerator.

2 Peel the shrimp and use a bamboo skewer to devein. Cut off the very tip of the shrimp tail and remove the water. Wash *satsuma-imo* with skin on, slice to 1 cm (0.4 in) wide on the diagonal. Wash *shiso* leaf and cut off the stem. Grate *daikon* and ginger and keep separate.

3 Pour enough oil into a pan and heat on medium heat (170°C / 340°F). Just before frying, make batter. Take A and B out of refrigerator and mix together very roughly. The oil is ready when you drop a small amount of batter into the pan and it fries quickly.

天ぷら

材料（4人分）
海老（約10cm）…8本
さつま芋…8切れ
大葉…8枚
衣
　A
　┌ 卵…1個
　└ 冷水…1カップ
　B
　┌ 薄力粉…½カップ
　└ 片栗粉…¼カップ
揚げ油…適宜
天つゆ…1カップ
大根おろし…½カップ
おろししょうが…大さじ1

作り方

1 衣の準備をする。Aをよく溶き混ぜる。別のボウルにBをよく混ぜ、それぞれ冷蔵庫で冷やす。

2 海老の背わたを取り、尾の先を切り、水けをしごき出す。さつま芋は1cm厚さの斜め切りにする。大葉は軸を切る。大根おろし、おろししょうがを用意する。

3 鍋に油をたっぷりと入れ、170℃に熱する。揚げる直前に、冷蔵庫でよく冷やしたAに少しずつBを加え、さっくりと、粉が残るくらいに混ぜ、衣を作る。衣少量を油に落としてすぐにかたまり、浮いてくれば適温。

4 Dip the *shiso* leaves into the batter on
one side, then gently slide the battered
side down into the oil and fry for about
30 seconds until light brown. Dip the
satsuma-imo into the batter and cover
the outside. Slide it into the oil and cook
for 3-4 minutes until medium brown.
Check by inserting a bamboo skewer
into it. If it comes out easily, it is done.
Dip shrimp into the batter by holding
its tail and then slide it into the oil and
cook for about 1 minute until the shrimp
changes to a white and red color.
Remove and place on a paper towel.

5 Transfer to a serving platter lined with
paper towels. Place grated *daikon* and
grated ginger and add *ten-tsuyu*.

Notes:

- Use a pan that has high sides and a smaller
base so that the oil doesn't splash up. Make
sure not to overcrowd the pan.
- Add salt and a slice of lemon on the side as
you like.

4 まず大葉の表側に衣を薄く
つけ、熱した油の中に衣の側
からそっと入れ、30秒ほど表
面がカリッとするまで揚げる。
次にさつま芋に衣をつけ、竹
串が通るまで、3〜4分揚げる。
最後に海老の尾を持って衣を
つけ、1分ほど背が赤くなるま
でさっと揚げる。それぞれキッ
チンペーパーの上に取り、油を
きる。

5 懐紙やキッチンペーパーなど
を敷いた皿に天ぷらを盛り合
わせ、天つゆと大根おろし、お
ろししょうがを添える。

作り方のコツ
天ぷら鍋は底が小さく高さのあ
るもののほうが、油の量が少な
くてすみ、油がはねにくい。油
の温度が下がるので、いっぺ
んにたくさん入れないこと。

好みで塩とレモンを添える。

Chapter 4

Home Cooking with Basic Seasonings

第四章

基本調味料でつくる
家庭料理

Miso Shiru

Miso shiru is made with *dashi* and *miso*, and is an essential part of a traditional *washoku*. Regional variations are based on different types of *miso* and ingredients used, such as *tofu* and seasonal vegetables or clams. The aroma of *miso* is very delicate and best when freshly cooked.

Ingredients————————————Serves 4

About 4 cups (1L) *dashi*
1/2 *momen* **(firm)** *tofu*
1/5 cup *wakame* **(dried seaweed)**
About 1/5 cup *miso*
5cm (2 in) *naganegi* **leek**

1 Drain water from *momen tofu* and cut into 2 cm (4/5 in) cubes.

2 Soak *wakame* in cold water and drain. If needed, cut *wakame* into 2 cm (0.8 in) strips. Cut *naganegi* in half and remove bitter center. Slice thinly.

3 Reheat *dashi* in a saucepan on medium heat. When it starts to boil, add *tofu* for 1 minute. Add *miso* by placing in a ladle with some *dashi* and stirring to dissolve before adding to the saucepan. Add *wakame*, and then quickly turn off heat.

4 Serve soup in small, individual bowls and garnish with *naganegi*.

Notes:
- To make *dashi* quickly, put packets of additive-free *dashi* into boiling water.
- For optimal flavor, do not boil soup after *miso* is added.

味噌汁

だしを沸かして味噌を溶き入れた、伝統的な和の食卓に欠かせない汁物。香りがとびやすい味噌は、煮えばなをいただきたい。具材は豆腐や旬の野菜、貝類など。味噌と具は、季節や地方によって変わる。

材料（4人分）
だし…約5カップ
木綿豆腐…½丁
わかめ（乾燥）…¼カップ
味噌…約¼カップ
長ねぎ…5㎝

作り方
1 豆腐は水をきり、2㎝角に切る。

2 わかめは水でもどし、2㎝長さに切る。長ねぎは縦半分に切って芯を除き、薄切りにする。

3 鍋にだしを沸かし、豆腐を加えて1分ほど煮、味噌をおたまで溶き入れる。わかめを加えてすぐに火を止める。

4 椀によそい、ねぎを添える。

作り方のコツ
だしは、沸いた湯にだしパックを入れて煮出してもよい。

味噌は香りがとびやすいので、溶き入れてから再び沸いたらすぐに火を止めること。

Gohan

Gohan (cooked rice) is a staple of *washoku*, and preparing rice is a fundamental skill to learn in Japanese cooking. Traditionally, rice is boiled in a *donabe* (clay pot) to cook the grains evenly and release a pleasant aroma.

Ingredients———————————Serves 4

1 2/3 cups *kome* (Japanese rice)
1 2/3 cups (400ml) water

1 Measure *kome* with a measuring cup and put into a large bowl. Pour plenty of water over *kome*, rinse once, and drain most of the water.

2 Wash *kome* (your hand should look as if you are holding a ball) by moving your hand in a clockwise motion and then stopping at the original position where you started. Repeat 10 times per cup of *kome*. Drain cloudy water, add water again, and repeat this rinsing process 3 times. Add water and soak *kome* for 10 minutes. Drain the water and let stand in a strainer for 15 minutes.

3 Put *kome* into a *donabe* and add the same amount of water as *kome*. Cover and bring to a slow boil over high heat. When it starts steaming, open cover and stir well from the bottom of the pot. Cover and cook on low heat for another 8-10 minutes. Remove from heat and leave covered for 10 minutes.

4 Mix *gohan* with a *shamoji* (rice paddle) or wooden spoon to fluff it up.

Notes:
- If using a rice cooker, use the rice and water measurements for your rice cooker. Then follow steps #1, 2, and 4.
- This recipe is for *shinmai* (rice fresh from harvesting). Add slightly more water for older rice.

ごはん

毎日炊いているごはんも、研ぎ方に気をつけるだけでおいしさが変わる。土鍋で炊けば、米一粒一粒が立った香ばしい炊き上がりが楽しめる。

材料（4人分）
米…2カップ
水…2カップ

作り方
1 ボウルに米2カップを入れ、たっぷりの水を注ぎ、ざっと混ぜて水を流す。

2 米1カップにつき10回研ぎ、たっぷりの水を注いで流す作業を3回繰り返す。水を入れ10分おいて浸水させ、ざるに上げて15分ほどおく。

3 土鍋に米を入れ、同量の水を注ぎ、ふたをして強火にかける。ふいてきたら、一度ふたを取って鍋の中の上下を返し、ふたをして弱火にし、8〜10分ほど加熱し、火を止め、10分蒸らす。

4 炊き上がったら、しゃもじで鍋の中を大きく返す。

作り方のコツ
炊飯器の場合は、機器の容量と指示に従う。

秋の新米の時期から月日とともに、米から徐々に水分が抜けていくので、水の量は適宜加減すること。

Teriyaki Swordfish

Teriyaki is a basic Japanese cooking technique for *yakimono* (grilled dish). *Teriyaki tare* (sauce) consists of *shoyu, sake,* and *mirin,* which imparts a sweet, salty flavor and its shine. This is a versatile sauce for seafood and chicken.

Ingredients———————— Serves 4

4 swordfish fillets
A
⌐ **2 Tbsp** *shoyu*
⎟ **2 Tbsp** *mirin*
⌞ **2 Tbsp** *sake*
Flour for sifting
1 tsp vegetable oil
8 pieces *shishito* **pepper**

1 Make *teriyaki* sauce. Stir A together and pour over swordfish, then marinate for 15 minutes.

2 Remove the excess moisture from the swordfish with a paper towel. Using a sifter, lightly dust the swordfish with flour on both sides.

3 Heat the oil in a pan on medium heat, then add #2. Pan-fry until lightly browned, turn over, and pan-fry the other side until both sides are brown and crispy. Add the rest of marinade sauce and cook until it becomes shiny. Remove swordfish and place on a serving platter.

4 Add the *shishito* peppers and quickly sauté over medium heat until they change to a bright green. Arrange on a serving platter.

Notes:
- Delicious with salmon, cod, or chicken.
- Grated ginger can be added to A to eliminate the fish smell.
- Pan-fry fish immediately after dusting with flour, and only turn fish over once to prevent breaking. The side pan-fried first will be placed upward on the plate.

かじきまぐろの照り焼き
照り焼きは、日本料理の甘辛い焼き物の基本。醤油、酒、みりんを同量合わせたたれを煮詰めて素材にからめることで、独特の甘辛さと照りがつく。魚貝類や鶏肉に応用できる。

材料（4人分）
かじきまぐろ…4切れ
A
⌐ 醤油…大さじ2
⎟ みりん…大さじ2
⌞ 酒…大さじ2
小麦粉…適宜
植物油…小さじ1
ししとう…8本

作り方
1 Aの材料を混ぜ合わせ、かじきまぐろを15分ほどAに浸ける。

2 キッチンペーパーでかじきまぐろから余分な水けを拭き取り、茶こしで小麦粉を両面に薄くふる。

3 フライパンに油を入れて中火で熱し、2を入れ、軽く焼き色がついたら裏返し、残った漬け汁を入れ、煮詰めながら照りを出す。皿に取る。

4 空いたフライパンにししとうを入れてさっと炒め、かじきまぐろに添える。

作り方のコツ
鮭、たら、鶏肉なども照り焼きにすると美味しい。

魚の臭みが気になるときには照り焼きのたれ（A）におろししょうがを加える。

粉をはたいてから、すぐにフライパンに入れること。焼くとき、ひっくり返すのは一度だけにし、先にフライパンに入れた面が盛り付けのときは表になる。

Saikyo-yaki Black Cod

Saikyo miso is a white, sweet *miso* from Kyoto. *Misozuke* is a traditional way of preserving fish by marinating in *miso* paste with *mirin* and *sake*. *Saikyo-yaki* is a significant type of *yakimono* (grilled dish).

Ingredients————————Serves 4

4 black cod fillets
1 Tbsp salt
A
⎡ **About 1/2 cup white *miso***
⎢ **About 1/2 cup brown *miso***
⎣ **4 Tbsp *sake***

1 Sprinkle salt onto both sides of the black cod fillets. Marinate for 15 minutes.

2 Stir A together until smooth.

3 Remove the excess moisture from the black cod with a paper towel. Spread ½ of A onto the bottom of a flat container big enough to hold the 4 fillets, place fish on top of A, and spread the other ½ of A on top. Cover and refrigerate overnight or for up to 2 days.

4 After marinating, gently scrape off the paste with a spatula. Preheat oven to 220°C (430°F) or use the broiler. A Japanese fish griller works best if available. Remove from oven and arrange fish on a serving dish.

Notes:

- Delicious with butterfish, salmon, or scallops.
- Grated ginger can be added to A to eliminate the fish smell.
- Be sure to remove all of the *miso* paste or it may burn. Baking/grilling time may differ depending on the thickness of the fish.

銀だらの西京焼き

西京焼きとは、京都の西京味噌（甘口の白味噌）にみりんや酒などを加えた味噌床に、魚の切り身を漬けて焼く料理。本来、魚の保存の手段として生まれた料理だが、品のいい甘みは、日本を代表する焼き物の一つに。

材料（4人分）
銀だら…4切れ
塩…大さじ1
A
⎡ 白味噌…約½カップ
⎢ 味噌…約½カップ
⎣ 酒…大さじ4

作り方
1 銀だらは両面に塩をふって、15分おく。

2 Aの材料を混ぜ合わせる。

3 1が4切れ並ぶ大きさの保存容器などに2の半量を敷き、1の水けを軽くぬぐって並べ、残りの2をかぶせ、2日ほど漬ける。

4 3を取り出して味噌をぬぐい、熱した魚焼きグリルか220℃に熱したオーブンでこんがりと色よく焼く。

作り方のコツ
まながつお、鮭、帆立てなども西京焼きに向く。

魚の臭みが気になるときには味噌床（A）におろししょうがを加える。

こげないよう、味噌をとりのぞいてから焼く。焼き時間は魚の厚さによって加減する。

Nikujaga

Nikujaga is a popular Japanese *nimono* (simmered dish).
In the cooking process, sugar, salt, and *shoyu* are used in
the order of Japanese seasoning theory covered in Chapter 1.

Ingredients————————Serves 4

200 g (7 oz) very thinly-sliced beef
500 g (1lb) potatoes
1 Tbsp sliced ginger
1 Tbsp *goma* (sesame) oil
1 1/2 Tbsp sugar
3 Tbsp + 1 tsp *sake*
1 1/4 cups (300ml) water
1 1/2 Tbsp *shoyu*
6 *ingen* (French green) beans
Pinch of salt

1. Cut potatoes into 5 cm (2 in) x 5 cm chunks and soak potatoes in cold water for 5-10 minutes to remove the starch. Drain water and rinse with cold water.

2. Heat a pan on medium heat and pour in *goma* oil. Add ginger and sauté until fragrant. Add beef and sauté until seared, then add the potato chunks and continue to sauté. Sprinkle sugar over beef and potatoes and sauté until ingredients become shiny.

3. Slowly pour in water. Cover pan with lid and bring to a boil over high heat. Once boiling, scum will rise to the top. Using a spoon, carefully remove the scum. Add *sake*, cover, and simmer on low heat for 15 minutes.

4. While simmering #3, add water and salt to a saucepan and bring to a boil over high heat. Quickly parboil *ingen*, soak in cold water, and then drain. Once cool, slice *ingen* on the diagonal to 3 cm (1.2 in) in length.

肉じゃが

日本人なら誰もが好きな甘辛味の煮物。まず砂糖を加え、酒と水で煮、最後に醤油を加えるのが、少量の調味料で的確に調味するコツ。まさに、さ・し・す・せ・その原理。

材料（4人分）
牛薄切り肉…200g
じゃが芋…500g
しょうが（せん切り）…大さじ1
ごま油…大さじ1
砂糖…大さじ1 1/2
酒…1/4 カップ
水…1 1/2 カップ
醤油…大さじ1 1/2
いんげん…6本
塩…少々

作り方
1 皮をむいて5cm角に切ったじゃが芋は5〜10分水にさらし、でんぷんを除く。

2 鍋にごま油を入れて熱し、しょうがをさっと炒めて香りが立ったら牛肉を加え、色が変わるまで炒める。続いてじゃが芋を加え、砂糖をふり入れ、全体につやが出るまで炒める。

3 水を注いでふたをし、強火で煮る。沸いたらアクを取って酒を加え、火を弱めてふたをし、15分ほど煮る。

4 3を煮ている間に、別鍋でいんげんを塩ゆでし、冷水にとって冷ます。水をきり、長さ3cmの斜め薄切りにする。

5 Pour in *shoyu* at the end of cooking for its flavor. Remove cover and boil again on high heat for 3-5 minutes. Turn off heat and keep covered for about 2 hours. Before serving, quickly reheat on medium heat uncovered. Spoon into a big bowl and garnish with *ingen* beans. Serve into individual bowls to share.

Notes:
- *Nimono* should be cooled down first, then warmed up before serving. This process intensifies the flavors.

5 最後に醤油を加えて、ふたはせずに3〜5分強火で煮る。ふたをして常温に2時間ほどおく。食べる直前に、ふたをせず中火で温めて器に盛り、いんげんを散らす。

作り方のコツ
煮物は冷めるときに味が入るので、一度冷まし、食べるときに温めるとなお、味が深くなる。

Chirashi zushi

Chirashi zushi is a bowl of *sushi* rice covered with various types of *sashimi* (sliced raw fish and shellfish). To make *sushi meshi* (rice), mix *sushi zu* (vinegar) with *gohan*, then cool it down and allow to dry.

Sushi meshi
- 1 2/3 cups *kome* (Japanese rice)
- 1 1/2cups (360ml) water
- 5 cm (2 in) x 5 cm *konbu* (seaweed)

Sushi zu
- About 1/4 cup rice vinegar
- 2 1/2 Tbsp sugar
- 1 1/2 tsp salt

Kinshi Tamago (thin-sliced egg crepe)
  2 eggs

A
- 1 Tbsp sugar
- Pinch of salt
- 2 Tbsp *sake*
- 1 tsp *katakuriko* (potato starch)
- 1 tsp vegetable oil

Sashimi
  60g (2 oz) raw sea bream or any
  white-fleshed meat fish *sashimi*
  60g (2 oz) raw salmon or any
  red-fleshed fish *sashimi*
  8 pieces scallop *sashimi*

2 cucumbers
  1/2 tsp salt
1 sheet *nori* (dried seaweed)
2 Tbsp roasted *shiro goma* (white sesame seeds)
12 *shiso* (perilla) leaves

Condiments
Wasabi, *gari* (pickled ginger)

1 Make *sushi meshi*. Refer to the instructions for *gohan* (p.92). Reduce water 10% from usual rice cooking and add *konbu* for a rich flavor. Transfer *gohan* to a *handai* (traditional Japanese wooden rice bowl) or a large wooden salad bowl by spooning the rice into a pile in the center of the bowl. Stir together *sushi zu* ingredients until well combined, then pour onto a rice

ちらし寿司

寿司飯は酢に砂糖と塩を加えた寿司酢を炊き立てのごはんに手早く混ぜたもの。あおいで急冷し、水分をとばして仕上げる。あとは好みの魚貝などをのせるだけで上等なちらし寿司に。

材料（4人分）
寿司飯
- 米…2カップ
- 水…1 4/5 カップ
- 昆布…5cm角1枚

寿司酢
- 米酢…約1/3カップ
- 砂糖…大さじ2 1/2
- 塩…小さじ1 1/2

錦糸卵
  卵…2個

A
- 砂糖…大さじ1
- 塩…ひとつまみ
- 酒…大さじ2
- 片栗粉…小さじ1
- 植物油…小さじ1

刺身
  鯛（白身魚）…60g
  鮭（赤身魚）…60g
  帆立て貝柱…8個分

きゅうり…2本
  塩…小さじ1/2
のり…1枚
白煎りごま…大さじ2
大葉…12枚

薬味
わさび、ガリ

作り方
1 寿司飯を作る。ごはんの炊き方（p.92）を参考に、寿司飯は通常より1割程度水加減

paddle and drizzle all over the *gohan*. Quickly mix well and then use an *uchiwa* (small handheld fan) to cool the mixture. Continue this process for a few minutes. Cover with a slightly damp kitchen cloth and let the *sushi meshi* sit for 10 minutes.

2　Make *kinshi tamago*. Stir eggs first, then add A and stir together. Add oil to a small frying pan or crepe pan on low heat. Pour ¼ of the mixture into pan and spread evenly by turning the pan to form a thin layer. Cook the egg for 1 minute, then remove the pan from the stovetop. Wait for another minute until well-cooked by the remaining heat. Remove from pan and cool. Repeat 4 times, then cut the layers of egg into thin slices lengthwise.

3　Cut cucumber in half lengthwise and remove the seeds with a small spoon. Slice very thinly into moon shapes and sprinkle with salt. Gently squeeze the cucumber to remove moisture.

4　Make *sashimi*. Slice raw fish into pieces 1 cm (0.4 in) thick. Slice raw scallop into 3 thin pieces.

5　Hand-cut *nori* into tiny pieces. Add *nori* and *shiro goma* to *sushi meshi* and gently fold the rice to combine.

6　Place #5 into 4 separate bowls and arrange the *sashimi* beautifully on top with *shiso* leaves. Place *kinshi tamago* and cucumber. Serve immediately with *wasabi* and/or *gari* as you like. Use *shoyu* for dipping.

Notes:
- Use raw fish and vegetables that create a variety of contrasting colors and textures to enhance the look and taste. Precut *sashimi* can be used easily.
- Serve with freshly grated *wasabi* if available or replace to *yuzu-kosho*.

を減らし、昆布を入れて炊く。寿司酢の材料をよく混ぜ、飯台に移しておいたごはんに回しかけ、しゃもじで切るように上下を返し、うちわであおいで一気に冷ましながら混ぜる。ぬれ布巾をかぶせ、10分ほどおく。

2　錦糸卵を作る。卵を溶きほぐし、Aを加え混ぜ、油を入れて温めたフライパンに1/4量ずつ流し、薄焼き卵を作る。約1分ほど焼いたら、フライパンを火からはずし、もう1分ほどおき余熱で火を通す。同様に4枚の薄焼き卵を作り、重ねてせん切りにする。

3　きゅうりは縦半分に切り、小さいスプーンで種を除き、薄切りにして塩をまぶし、しんなりしたら水けを絞る。

4　刺身を用意する。魚を約1cm厚さに切りそろえ、帆立貝柱は三枚に切る。

5　小さくちぎったのりとごまを、寿司飯にさっくり混ぜる。

6　それぞれの器に5をよそい、刺身類を大葉とともに彩りよく盛る。錦糸卵、きゅうりを盛り込み、好みでわさびやガリを添える。醤油（分量外）をつけて食べる。

作り方のコツ
刺身類と付け合わせの野菜は、好みのものを彩りと味の対比を考えて選ぶ。出来合いの刺身を利用してもいい。

わさびはすりおろしたばかりのものがよいが、なければゆず胡椒を添えてもいい。

Glossary

Author's Choice

付録

用語集
おすすめ商品

Glossary | 用語集

Ki-re

Ki-re refers to sweetness that vanishes from the mouth immediately. If a flavor has *ki-re*, it has a clear, crisp aftertaste and resonance. However, this term also sometimes corresponds to the English concept of "dryness" when referring to beverages like beer with a sharp finish.

Koku

Koku refers to rich, strong, or heavy flavors imparted by ingredients like oils, fats, sugars, and *umami*. *Koku* is the opposite of a light taste.

Caramelization

Heating sugar will gradually cause it to melt. At temperatures over 160°C (320°F), sucrose will continually break apart and recombine, undergoing an oxidation reaction that turns sugar brown. This process gives sugar a fragrant aroma and gentle bittersweet flavor, and this change in sugar is referred to as "caramelization." Confectioners often use caramelized sugar as a sauce or for added flavor.

キレ

口の中にある甘みが、すっと切れてなくなり、あとに残らないかどうかをいう。キレがいいとは、あと味、余韻がすっきりしていること。一方、ビールなどの飲み物では、辛口でのど越しシャープな様子を指す場合もある。

コク

油脂分や旨み分、糖分などの働きで、味わいに重みや強さ、豊かさなどが加わった状態を、コクがあるという。軽やかな味わいの反対。

カラメル化

砂糖を加熱していくと、次第に砂糖が溶けてくる。160℃を超えると、蔗糖（しょとう）（砂糖の主成分）自体が分解や結合を繰り返し、酸化反応をおこして褐色へと変化する。その過程で、砂糖は香ばしい香りやほろ苦みを伴うが、この変化のことをカラメル化という。製菓用にはカラメル化した砂糖をソースや風味づけによく用いる。

Enden

The *Enden* is a salt pan that uses sunlight and wind to evaporate seawater, producing salt or concentrated brine. In places like Australia where there's little rain and lots of sunshine, sunlight alone can be used to crystalize salt for solar salt production. However, most Japanese salt pans heat concentrated brine in order to crystallize salt.

One of the two most representative approaches is the "*irihama*" method of the *Seto* Inland Sea region. In this method, the ebb and flow of the tides is used to redirect seawater. In contrast, the "*agehama*" method of the *Noto* Peninsula is more complex. It involves dousing beach sand with salt water, repeatedly mixing it as the sunshine and wind evaporate moisture, and then gathering the salt sand. The sand is then washed with seawater, and the results are simmered in a pot to crystalize the salt.

塩田

太陽熱や風で海水の水分を蒸発させ、塩、あるいは製塩の原料（濃縮鹹水）をとるための設備。オーストラリアなどのように雨が少なく日照時間の長い地域では、太陽光のみで塩を結晶させる天日塩がつくれるが、日本の塩田の多くは何らかの形で海水を濃縮した鹹水を加熱して結晶を得ている。

代表的なものに、砂浜の上に海水をまき、頻繁にかき混ぜながら天日と風により水分を蒸発させ、塩砂を集めて海水で洗い、その後釜で煮詰めて結晶を得る能登の揚げ浜式塩田や、潮の満ち干を利用して海水を導き入れる瀬戸内の入り浜式塩田がある。

Shiomomi

Shiomomi is a type of preparation method in which ingredients (usually vegetables) are dusted with salt and massaged. This method uses the salt to remove moisture. Dusting with salt and massaging vigorously also effectively removes hairy fibers from vegetable surfaces, like those of *edamame* and *okra*. Additionally, *shiomomi* can help keep vegetables colorful after boiling.

Tsukemono

Tsukemono have a long shelf life and a fragrant, well-aged flavor. *Tsukemono* are usually made from vegetables pickled in salt, *miso*, or *nuka* (rice bran). Some varieties of *tsukemono* also undergo lactic acid fermentation, further enhancing their flavor. This is thanks to the sugars and bacteria present in them. Every region of Japan has its own methods and ingredients for pickling. Moreover, all of these *tsukemono* are beloved in their areas as accompaniments to staples like rice and other grains. As local flavors, all of these varieties have an important role in the transmission of food culture.

塩もみ

主に野菜などに塩をまぶして手でもむことによって、塩の浸透圧で脱水させる下処理の手法をいう。枝豆やオクラなど、表面に産毛のある食材は、塩をまぶしてよくもむことで、産毛を取り除くという効果もある。また、塩でもむことで、色鮮やかにゆで上がるというメリットもある。

漬け物

日本の漬け物は、主に野菜を、塩、味噌、糠などで漬け込み、保存性を高めるとともに、熟成させて風味をよくした食品。漬け物の種類によっては、素材が持っている乳酸菌と素材に含まれる糖類によって乳酸発酵が促され、より風味が向上するものもある。日本各地にさまざまな手法による漬け物が存在するが、いずれも、主食である米などの穀物の副菜として愛されてきたもので、郷土の味として、食文化を伝える役割を担っている。

Kakushi-aji

Kakushi-aji refers to a technique where a single seasoning (e.g., sugar, vinegar, soy sauce, etc.) is added to a dish. The *kakushi-aji* contrasts with the finished dish's flavor, and is added in an amount too small to notice when served. This produces a clear improvement in flavor. The term can also refer to the seasoning used, specifically. Examples include adding a little salt to heighten sweetness, or adding a little vinegar to a simmered dish. Sometimes these combination of flavors can be quite surprising, like adding a touch of chocolate to a curry.

隠し味

料理を食べたときに、よりはっきりと美味しいと感じてもらうために、本来の味つけの方向性にはない少量の砂糖、酢、醤油などを、単体の味としては気づかれない程度の量を加えるテクニックのこと。またはその調味料。甘みを際立たせるために塩少量を加えたり、煮物に酢少量を加えるなどはその例。カレーにチョコレートを少量加えるといった、意外なものを加える場合にもいう。

Koji

Many Japanese seasonings are made by fermenting grains with *koji*, a domesticated fungus. These can include vinegar, soy sauce, *miso*, *sake*, and *mirin*. *Koji* is bred from the mold Aspergillus oryzae using soybeans or cereals like wheat and rice.

As an example, soy sauce is made by letting A. oryzae grow on steamed soybeans and wheat and adding salt water. The resulting *moromi* is allowed to ferment and age, then soy sauce is squeezed from it. For *miso*, steamed soybeans are mixed in with *koji* (there are three types: rice, wheat, and soybean *koji*), salted, and left to ferment. When making *sake*, A. oryzae is allowed to grow on steamed rice to create rice *koji*. Next, the *koji* and steamed rice are mixed with water and yeast and allowed to ferment, creating alcohol.

In all of these cases, *koji* breaks down the starches and proteins in the steamed rice or wheat to create amino acids. Over time, the combined ingredients transform into delicious seasonings through *koji*'s assistance.

麹

酢、醤油、味噌、酒、みりん、日本の調味料はいずれも、原料である穀物を麹で発酵させることによってつくられている。麹とは米、麦、大豆などの穀類に麹菌を繁殖させたもの。つまり、麹をつくる元の元が麹菌である。

例えば醤油は、蒸した大豆と小麦に麹菌をつけ、塩水を加えて発酵させ、熟成したもろみを搾ったもの。味噌は蒸した大豆に麹（米麹、麦麹、豆麹と3種ある）と塩を加えて発酵させる。酒であれば、蒸した米に麹菌をつけて米麹をつくり、その麹に、蒸し米、水、酵母を合わせてアルコール発酵させて搾る。

いずれも、発酵の過程で麹は蒸米や蒸し麦のでんぷんやたんぱく質を分解してたくさんのアミノ酸を生成し、時間をかけて美味しい調味料へと変化させていく。そのプロセスを支えているのが麹なのである。

Moromi

Moromi is a mash produced in the process of making *sake* or soy sauce. When the ingredients are fully fermented but not yet drained of liquids, they are a *moromi*. Soy sauce *moromi* is fragrant, rich, and delicious, so it can be used as a seasoning in and of itself. The type of *miso* called "*moromi miso*" is actually more similar to the mash from soy sauce than it is to *miso*, making it a cousin of dishes like *kinzanji miso*.

Umami

Umami describes the delicious taste of savory flavor essences. For many years, people held to the belief that humans can taste only five basic flavors (sweet, sour, salty, bitter, and spicy) until a Japanese chemist discovered a sixth flavor in the early 20th century. Glutamic acid in tomatoes and seaweed, inosinic acid in *katsuobushi* and meats, succinic acid in shellfish, guanylic acid in *shiitake* mushrooms - many ingredients contain a wide variety of *umami* essences. In combination, they create a synergistic effect which produces an even more potent savory flavor.

もろみ

酒や醤油などの醸造の過程で、発酵は充分に進んでいるが、まだ液体分を漉し取っていない状態をもろみという。醤油のもろみの場合は、香り高くコクがあって美味しいので、それ自体を調味料として使用することもある。もろみ味噌と呼ばれる味噌は、味噌というよりも醤油もろみに近似したもので、金山寺味噌もそのジャンル。

旨み

食べたときに強く、美味しさを感じる、旨み成分を伴う味。長らく、甘、酸、塩、辛、苦の五味が人間の感じる味覚と思われていたが、20世紀初頭に日本人の化学者が第六の旨みを発見。昆布やトマトのグルタミン酸、かつお節や肉類のイノシン酸、貝類のコハク酸、椎茸のグアニル酸など、多くの素材に多彩な旨み成分が含まれていて、それらは二つが合わさると、相乗効果でより強い旨みとして感じられる。

Kinzanji Miso

A type of *miso* eaten on top of rice or as a snack with *sake*. *Kinzanji miso* is said to have been brought to Japan by a monk returning from Song-dynasty China. This *miso* is made by mixing a blend of chopped, roasted soybeans, *mugi* (barly)-*koji*, and salt together with vegetables like eggplant and ginger. The mixture is then left to age. It's said that the first soy sauces were skimmed off the top of *kinzanji miso*, or perhaps came from the liquid left at the bottom of the barrels it was stored in.

Aburu

This technique involves exposing ingredients to direct heat to cook or dry them. Traditionally this was done over an open charcoal flame, but nowadays it's quite common to use a gas flame.

金山寺味噌

ごはんにのせて、また酒の肴として食べる、なめ味噌の一種で、宋から戻った僧が伝えたといわれる。炒った大豆の引き割り、麦麹、塩を合わせ、なすやしょうがなどの野菜を混ぜて、熟成させたもの。金山寺味噌の上澄みや樽の底に残った液体が醤油のもとになったといわれる。

炙る

直火にかざして焼いたり乾かしたりする調理法。元来は炭の上で行うことが多かったが、現在ではガス火で炙る場合も多い。

Maillard Reaction

The Maillard reaction occurs when food is heated or fermented. The sugars and amino acids inside react with one another, producing a brown coloration as well as a variety of aromas and chemicals that impart flavor. Results of the Maillard reaction include grill marks on meat, its mouth-watering aroma, and the rich brown color of soy sauce.

Suimono

This term refers to the soup dishes of Japanese cuisine, generally made with a *dashi* broth of *katsuobushi* or *konbu* flavored with a touch of light soy sauce and salt. Common ingredients include seasonal vegetables and seafood, eggs, and fish cakes. However, the type of soup called "*wan-mono*" that appears among the courses of traditional Japanese *kaiseki* cuisine can resemble *suimono* at a glance. Even so, it is often a much more substantial and sumptuous offering that's treated like a main dish. Chefs take great care in its preparation, and it may include ingredients like *shinjo* (special fish cakes).

メイラード反応

食材を加熱したり、熟成させることで、食材の中にある糖とアミノ酸が反応して茶色く色づき、同時にさまざまな香りや成分を生む反応のこと。肉を焼くと、美味しそうな焦げ目がついていい香りが漂うのも、醤油がこっくりとした茶色を呈するのも、メイラード反応の一つである。

吸い物

日本料理における汁物の総称。主にかつお節と昆布で引いただしに、塩と薄口醤油少々で味をつける。具材は季節の野菜や魚貝類、卵、練り物など。ただし、懐石料理のコースの中で出される椀物は、大ぶりの吸い物のように見えるが、日本料理においては、主菜の位置づけとなる華やかな料理で、椀だねはしんじょう（魚のすり身を加工したもの）など、手のこんだ、大きなものになることが多い。

Dengaku

Dengaku is a dish of *tofu*, *konnyaku* (konjac), or vegetables like potato or eggplant skewered, coated with a *miso*-based sauce, and grilled on an open flame. The dish boasts a long history, and reportedly was already eaten widely by the *Muromachi* period (1336–1573 AD). Its name was drawn from the skewered ingredients' resemblance to the performers of a traditional rice-planting dance called "*dengaku-mai*." Dancers in this style utilize one-legged stilts.

Zoni

This is a type of *mochi* rice cake soup served hot during the New Year's holiday to celebrate. The ingredients, soup, and type of *mochi* vary substantially by region. Differences include soy sauce- or *miso*-based broths, *mochi* shapes (round or square), and whether the *mochi* is grilled or not. The ingredients may also feature regional specialties, such as local tubers, seafood, and vegetables.

田楽

豆腐やこんにゃく、また、なすや芋などの野菜を串に刺し、味噌ベースのたれを塗って直火で焼き上げる料理。歴史は古く、室町時代には広く食べられていたという。串刺しの形が、田植えのときに1本足の竹馬に乗って舞う田楽舞に似ていたことから、田楽と呼ばれるようになったという。

雑煮

新年を祝って正月に食べる、餅を入れた熱い汁物。餅、汁、具材とも、地方によって大きく異なる。まず、つゆの味つけは醤油ベースと味噌ベースに分かれ、餅も丸餅、角餅、焼いて入れる、焼かずに入れるなどの違いがある。具材も、芋類、魚介、野菜など、その地方ならではの特産品が入る。

Shitazawari

This is the Japanese expression for how something feels when it touches the tongue. Textures that are smooth (viscous, creamy, etc.) are "good" *shitazawari*, while rough and grainy textures are "bad" *shitazawari*. This is unlike *hazawari*, an expression for the texture of food when bitten - crunchy or crispy, etc.

Maroyaka

The term *maroyaka* describes a rounded and mild flavor that doesn't have any sharpness in its taste profile. *Maroyaka* is often experienced in dishes thickened with something like *ankake* starch sauce, in foods with a mild and gentle flavor from small amounts of sugar or milkfat. People often note *maroyaka* flavor in food with a rich variety of *umami* components.

Tare

Tare is a compound flavoring agent made with a base like soy sauce. As a sauce that brings something new to the taste of a dish, *tare* can be used to give a flavorsome coating to ingredients during simmering or grilling, added right before eating prepared dishes, and more.

舌触り

舌に感じる、感覚の表現。ねっとり、とろりなど、主になめらかであることを舌触りが良いといい、ざらつくなどは悪いといわれている。これに比して、歯触りというのは噛んだときの食感で、カリカリ、コリコリなどを指す。

まろやか

味覚としてとがったところのない、丸みのある穏やかな味わいを指す。あんかけのようにとろみがついていたり、少量の糖分や乳脂肪分による柔和な味つけをいう。人は、豊富な旨み成分などにまろやかさを感じることが多い。

たれ

醤油などをベースにつくる、複合調味料。煮たり焼いたりする加工調理の際に塗って味をつけたり、調理した食品につけて食べるなど、料理に味をプラスするためのもの。

Teri

Heating a blended seasoning that includes *mirin* or sugar results in a glaze that gradually thickens. This gives the dish a bright, shiny coating. This phenomenon is called "*teri*" in Japanese. You can also create a *teri* glaze by coating fish with *mirin* directly, then grilling.

Shochu

A general term for Japanese style of distilled alcohol made in *Kyushu* and the islands of *Okinawa* since the 16th century. A variety of ingredients are used in its production, such as *satsuma-imo* sweet potato, rice, barley, chestnuts, and *koku-tō*. *Shochu* came to Japan from the Kingdom of Siam (Thailand), according to the most prominent theory regarding its origins. From there, it passed through *Okinawa* to arrive in *Kyushu*. The many different ingredients used to create *Shochu* grant its varieties a wealth of character.

Kabayaki

This is a type of *teriyaki* dish where fish like eels, conger eels, and loaches are dressed and the heads are removed. They are then skewered, brushed with a mixed-ingredient

照り

みりんや砂糖を加えた合わせ調味料を熱すると、次第に濃度が出て、全体がテカりをおびて輝いてくる。その現象を照りが出るという。焼き魚などの仕上げに直接みりんを塗って焼き、照りを出すこともある。

焼酎

日本在来の蒸留酒の総称。九州と沖縄の島々で16世紀頃からつくられてきた。原料にはさつま芋、米、麦、栗、黒糖などが用いられる。来歴は、シャム王国（タイ）から、沖縄を経て、九州に上陸したという説が有力。原料の違いで香りも味わいもさまざまで個性豊か。

蒲焼き

うなぎ、穴子、どじょうなどの魚の頭を落として開き、串を打ってから、醤油、みりん、酒などを合わせたたれをつけ、直火で炙りながら焼く照り焼きの一種。最も有名な

glaze (for example, *tare* made from soy sauce, *mirin*, and *sake*), then grilled over an open flame. The most famous *kabayaki* dish is eel *kabayaki*, a signature dish of the *Edo* period. The "*kaba*" in "*kabayaki*" is thought to refer to the cattail; this is because a skewered, grilled eel looks a little bit like the plant's tail.

Tsuyu

Tsuyu is a compound flavoring agent made by adding *dashi* to a mixture of soy sauce, *mirin*, *sake*, and sugar. It is mainly used as a dipping sauce for noodles and *tempura*, or as a broth for *nabe*. Though similar to *tare* as a mixed seasoning, *tsuyu* is often used in larger quantities.

Chapter 3

Kaeshi

Kaeshi is used as a base for *soba tsuyu*. It is made by allowing soy sauce, sugar, and *mirin* to ferment for a short period after heating. Alternately, it can be made by fermenting the mixture for a longer period without heating to make soy sauce's flavor milder. At *soba* restaurants, *kaeshi* is diluted with *dashi* and served as *soba-tsuyu*. For hot *soba*, *kaeshi* is diluted with an increased ratio of *dashi*.

のがうなぎの蒲焼きで、江戸を代表する料理の一つだ。蒲焼きの「蒲」は、串に刺して焼いている姿が蒲の穂に似ていることから付いたという説がある。

つゆ

醤油、みりん、酒、砂糖にだしを加えてつくる、複合調味料。主に麺類をつける麺つゆ、天ぷらをつける天つゆのほか、鍋の煮汁などにも用いる。同じ合わせ調味料でも、たれに比べ、たっぷりと量を使う場合が多い。

第三章

かえし

そばつゆの素。醤油、砂糖、みりんを合わせて加熱した後、一定期間ねかせたもの、または、加熱せずに長期間ねかせ醤油の風味をまろやかにしたものをいう。そば屋ではこのかえしをだしで割って、そばつゆとして供する。つゆをたっぷりかけるかけそばでは、希釈するだしの割合を増やす。

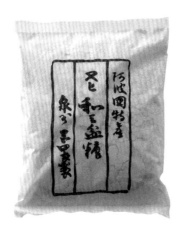

Awa Wasanbon Toh

Okada Sugar Manufacture
http://www.wasanbon.co.jp/

Iwatonoshio

Iwatokan
http://www.iwatokan.com/

阿波和三盆糖
岡田製糖所
徳島産さとうきびのエキスを搾って煮
詰めた後、水を加えて練り、圧を加え
て糖蜜を搾り出す作業を繰り返して
仕上げる。まろやかな甘み。

岩戸の塩
岩戸館
伊勢神宮沖の伏流水と海水のまじり
合う水を汲み出し、鉄釜に入れて薪
火で煮詰め、甘みが出るまで焼き上
げて仕上げたミネラル分豊かな塩。

Akou no Amashio

Amashio
http://www.amashio.co.jp/

Junyonesu

Yokoi Vinegar Brewing
http://www.yokoi-vinegar.co.jp/

赤穂の天塩
天塩
世界自然遺産の海、オーストラリア・
シャークベイの天日塩（塩田で自然に
結晶化した塩）とにがりを原料に結
晶した粗塩。

純米酢
横井醸造
国産米を原料にまず酒を醸し、種酢
（酢酸菌）を加えて丹念につくり上げ
る純米酢。米由来の自然な甘みで酸
味が柔らかい。

Usumurasaki

Kidishouyu
http://kidisyouyu.com/

Yuki-marudaizu no Ginsen-shoyu

Yamasa Corporation
http://www.yamasa.com/

うすむらさき
きち醤油
大豆：小麦：食塩水＝1：1：1という
一般的な濃口醤油の原料より小麦の
割合を増やして、発酵期間を短くし
て色を淡く抑えた淡口醤油。

ヤマサ特選有機丸大豆の
吟選しょうゆ
ヤマサ醤油
有機栽培の丸大豆、小麦、天日塩で
仕込み、約半年かけて熟成させる本
醸造醤油。

Tsuyahomare Miso

Koujiya Shibata Haruji Shoten
http://www.koujiyamiso.co.jp/

Inaka Miso

Koujiya Shibata Haruji Shoten
http://www.koujiyamiso.co.jp/

つやほまれみそ
糀屋柴田春次商店
米麹：蒸した大豆＝1：1で仕込む、
ほのかに甘口のふくよかな味わいの
米味噌。岐阜・飛騨高山で代々味噌
づくりを続ける専門店の品。

いなか味噌
糀屋柴田春次商店
蒸した大豆に麹菌をつけて大豆麹を
つくり、他方、蒸した大麦に麹菌をつ
けて麦麹をつくる。この二つを合わせ
て食塩水を加え、1年半熟成。

Kinjirushi Kizakura

Kizakura
http://kizakura.co.jp/

Fukuraijun San-nen Jukusei Honmirin

Hakusen Shuzou
http://www.hakusenshuzou.jp/

金印黄桜
黄桜
酒どころ、京都・伏見に創業。淡麗旨口の「金印黄桜」は、調和のとれたふくらみのある味わいと、豊かな香りが特徴の、黄桜を代表する一本。

福来純三年熟成本みりん
白扇酒造
飛騨産のもち米「たかやまもち」を蒸し、手作業で育てた米麹を加え、さらに自社製の米焼酎を加えて糖化させ、3年間熟成させてつくる。

Goma Neri-neri Kuro

Yamada Seiyu
http//henko.co.jp

Goma Neri-neri Shiro

Yamada Seiyu
http//henko.co.jp

ごまねりねり（黒）

山田製油　京都山田のへんこ
黒ごまを焙煎して石臼で挽いた、コク
のある黒の練りごま。あえ物のたれの
ほか、ごま豆腐や菓子類にも重宝。

ごまねりねり（白）

山田製油　京都山田のへんこ
白ごまをブレンドし、丁寧に焙煎した
のち、石臼で二度挽きにしたもの。ご
まだれや煮物などに多用できる。

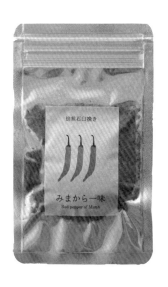

*Baisen Ishiusubiki
Mimakara Ichimi*

Haretoke Design Inc.
http://haretoke-d.jp/

*Ishiusubiki Sansho Powder
Kaori-sansho*

**Kaneichi Yamamoto-
Katsunosuke Syoten**
http://yamamotokatsunosuke.com/

焙煎石臼挽き みまから一味

ハレとケデザイン舎
糖度も辛みも強い徳島産のみまから
唐辛子を一定量ずつ焙煎し、旬の時
期に乾燥、ゆっくりと石臼で挽いた一
味唐辛子。

石臼挽き山椒粉 香山椒

かねいち山本勝之助商店
紀州特産の大粒ぶどう山椒を収穫
後、乾燥させ、昔ながらに石臼で挽
いて粉末にしたもの。柑橘系の香りと
しびれる辛みが特徴。

Koboku Yuzu-gosho

Kanetoshi
http://www.kanetoshi.co.jp/

Ginjou Nama-kanzuri 6nen-jikomi

Kanzuri
http://kanzuri.com/

枯木ゆずごしょう

カネトシ
種から育つ実生の枯木柚子を使用。
粗みじんに刻んだ青柚子の皮と青唐
辛子を粗くすりつぶし、塩を加え、柚
子果汁を加えて熟成。

吟醸生かんずり6年仕込み

かんずり
肉厚の新潟産唐辛子を天然海水塩
で塩漬け。その後、雪の上に蒔いて
さらし、アクを抜いた後、米麹、柚子、
塩を合わせて漬け込む。

松田美智子　まつだ・みちこ
料理研究家、テーブルコーディネーター、
女子美術大学講師。1993年より
松田美智子料理教室を主宰。
家庭で受け継がれた料理を大切にしながらも
科学の目を持ち、日々の暮らしを豊かに彩る
四季の味を教える。雑誌や広告の仕事に加え、
キッチンブランドの監修などでも活躍。
『いまどきのなべ』(文化出版局)、
『日本の味』(主婦と生活社)ほか著書多数。

鍋島徳恭　なべしま・なるやす
フォトグラファー。情感に溢れた独自の
世界観を持つ作品で広告・雑誌で幅広く活躍。
2006年より歌舞伎の伝統と中村吉右衛門の
芸を記録し、後世に残すため撮影を続けている。

小松宏子　こまつ・ひろこ
フードエディター。近刊に『ジビエ教本』
(依田誠志著／誠文堂新光社)。
『茶懐石に学ぶ日日の料理』
(後藤加寿子著／文化出版局)では
グルマン世界料理本大賞特別文化遺産賞受賞。
編著書多数。

英文翻訳
Active Gaming Media
レシピ英文執筆
Jeannine Law-Smith
装丁・本文デザイン
金田一亜弥　髙畠なつみ(金田一デザイン)

Bilingual Guide to Japan
WASHOKU SEASONING

和食調味料バイリンガルガイド

2016年12月25日　初版　第1刷発行

著　者　松田美智子
発行者　奥山豊彦

発行所　株式会社小学館
　　　　〒101 - 8001
　　　　東京都千代田区一ツ橋2 - 3 - 1
　　　　編集　03 - 3230 - 5119
　　　　販売　03 - 5281 - 3555
　　　　編集／矢野文子　販売／奥村浩一

印刷所　大日本印刷株式会社
製本所　株式会社若林製本工場